100 Smart Ways to Teach Mathematics

Part 1   For grade 1 to 8
Part 2   For high school and up

Chong An Chang

iUniverse, Inc.
Bloomington

100 Smart Ways to Teach Mathematics

iUniverse books may be ordered through booksellers or by contacting:

iUniverse
1663 Liberty Drive
Bloomington, IN 47403
www.iuniverse.com
1-800-Authors (1-800-288-4677)

Because of the dynamic nature of the Internet, any web addresses or links contained in this book may have changed since publication and may no longer be valid. The views expressed in this work are solely those of the author and do not necessarily reflect the views of the publisher, and the publisher hereby disclaims any responsibility for them.

Any people depicted in stock imagery provided by Thinkstock are models, and such images are being used for illustrative purposes only.
Certain stock imagery © Thinkstock.

ISBN: 978-1-4697-7380-3 (sc)
ISBN: 978-1-4697-7381-0 (ebk)

Printed in the United States of America

iUniverse rev. date: 02/15/2012

Dedication

This book is dedicated to the centenary birthday commemoration of my mother Mme. Qiao, Yuzhen.

Preface

This book represents my life-long teaching experience in three countries China, the USA, and Canada. I graduated from Peking University, China 1968 and was later awarded M.S and Ph.D degrees from the University of Pittsburgh, USA. In my Learning Center (1995 - 2010), I taught and tutored Canadian students at a wide range of levels and answered countless questions to help them study math and physics. Throughout my 40 years long-time front-line practice, a teaching style of *converting hard to easy* was developed.

This book "*100 smart ways to teach mathematics*" contains two parts, totally 100 sections. Each section discusses a different mathematics topic and introduces a special smart way of teaching. Part 1 contains treatments of basic arithmetic operations ($+-\times\div$), perimeter and area, fractions, decimals, Euclidean geometry, mean values, integers, factoring, introductory algebra, linear equation and more. Part 2 contains coupled linear equations, quadratic functions and equations, trigonometry, sequence and series, vectors, calculus (differentiation and integration) and more. Teachers teaching any grade course may find that *both* parts are useful. All mathematics theorems and formulas in this book are of course not invented or created by the author. The author merely introduces the smart ways of teaching, including many special and useful tips.

As the author I would thank my wife S.J for her great support, thank my former Peking University classmates Wang Caizhang, Min Ji and Cai Weili for helpful discussion on one topic, thank Stuart Pollock, Xue Qionghua and Zhu Weizong for their encouragement.

I hope that this book is useful for teachers teaching at various levels in schools, learning centers and education academies. The book may also provide a reference to students and parents. Comments and suggestions are welcome.

Chong An Chang, Ph.D

Ontario, Canada.

100 Smart Ways to Teach Mathematics

Part 1   (For grade 1 to 8)

Part 2   (for high school and up)

Part 1

(For grade 1 to 8)

Chapter 1
Basic Operations

1.1   Tips to add and subtract time

Spring finally arrives. Outside the classroom beautiful cherry flowers bloom. Winter snow is gone. With birds chirping and singing on the branches, butterflies dancing among flowers, this quiet town in North America is filled with the fresh smell of spring.

Everyone celebrates the coming of a new season. What a wonderful magic work has our Mother Nature done! During the attractive and miraculous season change, green gradually replaced white. Squirrels waked up, jump between trees. The day time becomes longer and longer. Students carry their backpacks, come to Dr.C Learning Center to receive greetings from the teacher.

Dr.C, the mathematics professor, congratulates everybody: "Spring is here, how time flies! Let us begin today by talking about the change of time. The addition and subtraction of time are different from usual number operations. Want to know the difference? Please try to find what time is 4 hours and 57 minutes after 10:48 AM. Thank you."

Little girl Sophia writes the following:

$$
\begin{array}{r}
1048 \\
+\ 457 \\
\hline
1505
\end{array}
$$

So her answer is 15:05 (3:05 pm).

"Is this answer correct?" says Dr.C. "Let us estimate. The starting time 10:48 is almost 11 o'clock in the morning. The time elapse 4 hours 57 minutes is about 5 hours. 5 hours after 11 AM is 4 pm. Hence Sophia's answer (about 3 pm) is somewhat wrong. She carried on digits in the usual way. Indeed 1 hour is 60 minutes, not 100 minutes."

"How can we avoid such an error?" Dr.C told the class a little secret: "Just deliberately separate the hours and the minutes *far away* from each other, then we can easily perform the calculation correctly. The tip is small but still helpful. When we separate hours and minutes we get the following expression:

$$
\begin{array}{r r}
10 & 48 \\
+ \quad 4 & 57 \\
\hline
14 & 105
\end{array}
$$

"Since 105 minutes mean 1 hour and 45 minutes, the final time 14:105 is equivalent to 15:45, or 3:45 pm. Once we write the hours and the minutes far from each other, the carry-on is no longer automatic. This small tip really works."

Next question is "what time is 4 hours 57 minutes *before* 10:48 AM?" This time students apply Dr.C's method, separate the hours far away from the minutes. Since 48 minutes are less than 57 minutes, Sophia and other students "borrow" 1 hour from the hours, then convert it into 60 additional minutes so that

$$
\begin{array}{r r}
10 & 48 \\
- \quad 4 & 57 \\
\hline
? &
\end{array}
\quad \longrightarrow \quad
\begin{array}{r r}
9 & 108 \\
- \quad 4 & 57 \\
\hline
5 & 51
\end{array}
$$

4

The result is 5:51 AM. With a small tip the calculation becomes easy.

Dr.C praises young Sophia and other students. He points out: "This small tip can also be applied to calculate questions with months, days, and hours. If we write down the numbers right next to each other we may carry on digits without thinking."

Finally Dr.C says: "There exist many small but useful tips similar to this one. To apply these tips in our daily life often helps us do things correctly and easily."

1.2 Hard or easy?

Today is Saturday. In the morning class Dr.C asked young students who had just learned addition and subtraction to do an exercise. He drew two diagrams on the white board, one triangle and one square. He then asked the students to fill in the blanks with appropriate numbers, such that along every straight line, the sum of the two ends was the same as the number given at the middle (example: 5 --- 7 --- 2, $5 + 2 = 7$).

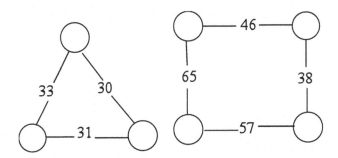

"Easy!" claimed the students. They started to calculate.

"Wait a moment please!" said Dr.C. "Before you start please first guess which question might be easier --- the triangle or the square?"

"The triangle!" most students immediately answered, because the triangle had one less side than the square.

"Also because the given numbers in the triangle are smaller than the given numbers in the square", said Teddy.

"However," said Linda, "I feel that the triangle might be harder, because I already found the answer of the square question."

Dr.C then encouraged the students not to stop after they found one answer. Continue; see whether it was possible to find the second, the third, and more answers to the same question.

Immediately they saw the difference!

With great surprise the students found that the square question was actually *much easier* than the triangle question! For the square you could start with almost any number, just went on and you would finish the whole question easily. When you started with different numbers you got different correct answers. It was so easy! On the other hand the triangle (although it looked easy) was indeed much harder, because there was only one set of possible answer. You had to place the number 16 on the top, then 14 and 17 clockwise. If you place another number on top, it would be impossible. Triangle question was harder because it only had one solution. If you did not find it, you had no answer at all.

Next, Dr.C drew a pentagon and a hexagon on the board, asked the students the same question: which one might be easier, the pentagon or the hexagon?

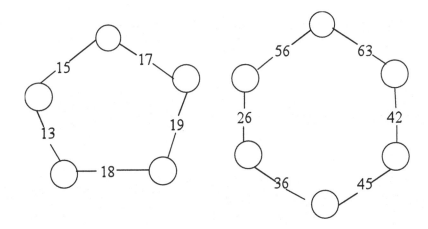

Again, the one which looked easier was actually much harder; the one which looked harder was actually much easier. The pentagon, with one side less than the hexagon, was harder because it only had one (the unique) solution. You had to place the number 9 on the top, otherwise it was impossible. However for the hexagon you could start with any number. If you knew negative numbers you might start with any number and got infinite groups of correct solutions. If you had not learned negative numbers you still had many solutions. To provide five or ten different answers was quite easy.

Dr.C then smiled and said: "In our daily life there are cases that a complicated thing is actually easy, an apparently easy thing may be actually difficult. Later when you learn how to solve coupled equations you will understand this more deeply. Let us now put down our pens and go out of the classroom, do some physical exercises and enjoy the beautiful spring atmosphere ..."

1.3   Estimation and smart calculation

Today the students were very active. Every student worked hard to compete with each other to play a game. Dr.C wrote the seven days of a week on the white board:

Sunday   *Monday*   *Tuesday*   *Wednesday*
Thursday   *Friday*   *Saturday*

Then he told the class: "Consider the English letter *a* as 1, *b* as 2, etc. until *z* as 26, please find the total value of a day by adding all numbers assigned to its letters. Tell me which day of a week is a lucky day. A lucky day is defined as the day with a total value of 100."

"Which day is a lucky day?   Is the student who can add numbers fastest the must-be winner? Not necessary!" said Dr.C.   "A smart way is to *estimate* the results first. If you feel that the total value of a day is probably too high (more than 100), or too low (much less than 100), then forget it and start with another day. Through this way you can find the answer without wasting much time. A student who calculates fast but tries many wrong days first will lag behind. A student who may not calculate as fast, but starts right with the correct day, will probably finish first. Another tip is to consider the part '*day*' as common to all words (with a value 4+1+25=30) to avoid unnecessary repetition in case you need to try other days."

Dr.C continued, gave the students more exercises: "In each question below the answer with a value of exactly 100 is considered as a 'lucky' answer. Each question only has one lucky answer."

[1] "Lucky animal" is
chicken   elephant   turtle   turkey   monkey

8

[2] "Lucky thing" is

television magazine newspaper dictionary telephone

[3] "Lucky place to work" is (a game only, do not be serious)

university library hospital government pharmacy

Estimation is only one way to speed up calculations. There are other ways. For example 29+17+71+33 can be evaluated by regrouping as $(29+71) + (17+33) = 100 + 50 = 150$.

Dr.C then asked the students to decode a secret message using $a = 1$, $b = 2$, etc. The answer is at the end of the chapter.

19 9 13 16 12 5   9 19   2 5 1 21 20 9 6 21 12

"In another question," Dr.C said, "it takes 5 hours for a bus to go from city A to city B or to go from city B to city A. At every hour on the hour one bus departures from A to B and one bus leaves B for A. If you sit in one of these buses and watch carefully --- you will see every oncoming bus, how many oncoming buses can you see during your trip?"

The answer to such a question could easily be thought as 5, since it took 5 hours for a city A bus to arrive at city B, and at every hour on the hour there was one bus leaving city B coming toward city A. However, Dr.C said: "Sorry, to answer 5 is incorrect. Just imagine that you leave city A at 6 AM, then you arrive at city B at 11 AM. At 6 AM while your bus departures, you see a bus arriving --- the 1 AM bus from city B. It left B at 1 AM and arrives at A at 6 AM. Five hours later at 11 AM when you arrive at city B, you see another city B bus just leaving. That is the scheduled 11 AM city B bus going toward city A.

"You meet the 1 AM city B bus and you meet the 11 AM city B bus, so you meet every city B bus between these two. What is the conclusion?

You meet all 11 buses during your 5-hour trip, not 5 buses, not 6 buses, but 11 buses inclusive. Isn't that surprising?"

1.4   Comments on subtractions

Mr. Frank, a good friend of Dr.C, teaches mathematics at a public school in the same city. He often discusses teaching methods with Dr.C. These days Mr. Frank teaches subtraction in his school. Subtraction is substantially more difficult than addition. Today Dr.C asked Mr. Frank how subtraction is taught in his school.

"As usual," said Mr. Frank. "I use the method illustrated in textbooks. I ask the students to cross out the digit. For example to do $24-7$, cross out the digit 2, change it to 1 and change that 4 to 14, then do $14-7$ first."

Dr.C said: "Your method is easy to learn for beginners, but it is complicated if the numbers become large. For instance if you calculate $63045-17289$, all digits of 63045 need to be crossed out and replaced by new numbers. 5 is less than 9 so we 'borrow' one from the digit 4 to do $15-9$. The number 4 now becomes 3 and we go on to cross out the 0, change 3 to 13 and do $13-8$, and so on, step by step.

$$
\begin{array}{r}
\overset{5}{\cancel{6}}\ \overset{\overset{12}{2}}{\cancel{3}}\ \overset{\overset{9}{10}}{\cancel{0}}\ \overset{\overset{13}{3}}{\cancel{4}}\ \overset{15}{\cancel{5}} \\
-\ 1\ 7\ 2\ 8\ 9 \\
\hline
4\ 5\ 7\ 5\ 6
\end{array}
$$

"The process is long and tedious. When the whole work is done, it is hard to read the original and it looks mess. Because of these reasons it is easy to make a mistake. Once a child learns a method, she or he will probably remember it and use it again and again for a whole lifetime, making it hard to change later in her or his life. At the same time the numbers involved in calculations will certainly grow greater and become more difficult.

"It is better to teach the students the method of 'dots'. Whether you put a dot on top of a digit or below it, the expression is much cleaner and simpler, especially for large number subtractions."

$$
\begin{array}{ccccc}
\dot{6} & \overset{\bullet}{3} & \dot{0} & \dot{4} & 5 \\
-\,1 & 7 & 2 & 8 & 9 \\
\hline
4 & 5 & 7 & 5 & 6 \\
\end{array}
\qquad
\begin{array}{ccccc}
6 & 3 & 0 & 4 & 5 \\
-\,\underset{\bullet}{1} & \underset{\bullet}{7} & \underset{\bullet}{2} & \underset{\bullet}{8} & 9 \\
\hline
4 & 5 & 7 & 5 & 6 \\
\end{array}
$$

Mr. Frank said: "I also tell my students when you do subtraction you can only do it from left to right. If you do addition, whatever order does not matter. When you do 18+8+4+3, you can do 8+4 first if you prefer. However, if you do $18-8-4-3$, you have to follow the order from left to right, cannot do $4-3$ (get 1) first then do $18-8-1$".

Dr.C agreed: "Yes, I would like to make a point. When we do subtraction between two similar, large numbers, the result is a much smaller number (such as $9873528-9873526=2$). If it is a practical measurement question in physics or engineering, the error in real life could be large and the result tends to be inaccurate.

1.5   Unnecessary calculations?

Dr.C randomly chose a number and wrote it on the board: 18.

Young kids in this class just learned the basic operations $(+,-,\times,\div)$. Dr.C said: "Please add 8 to the number 18, then subtract 8 from your result, then multiply 8 to the answer, and finally divide your new answer by 8. Please tell me what happens."

Tony raised his hand and said: "Dr.C, this is not necessary. We know that the answer is still 18; same as the number you gave us. Addition and subtraction, multiplication and division simply cancel each other."

"Excellent!" Dr.C praised young Tony. "Now, please read the following questions carefully. Do we really need to calculate each problem step by step, or we can just say that the answer is the same as the given number, there is no calculation necessary?

[1] Multiply 18 by 4, then subtract 4 from the answer, then divide the result by 4, and finally add 4 to the answer. (This is expressed as 18×4, -4, $\div 4$, finally $+4$.)

[2] $18+4$, $\times 4$, $\div 4$, finally -4.

[3] $18-4$, $\times 4$, $+4$, finally $\div 4$

[4] $18\div 3$, $+4$, -4, finally $\times 3$"

Soon the students found that questions [2] and [4] really did not require calculations step by step, operations simply cancelled each other and the final answer was still 18.   However, the answer of question [1] was 21 and the answer of question [3] was 15, different from the starting number 18.

Dr.C encouraged the students to study the questions thoroughly.

"Here is why!" cheered the students. "In these questions, in order to cancel one step the opposite calculation must follow that step immediately. There should be no gap. Inserting anything between the two would break the cancellation and a different result yields. If we obey this rule (even with different numbers like the 3 and 4 in [4]), the answer will remain unchanged; whereas if this rule is not obeyed, the answer will be different and each step of calculation is necessary."

1.6 Patterns

Sarah, Nadine and Dominic are learning how to find the hidden patterns in a set of given numbers. Sometimes this is easy --- the pattern is obvious. For example 1, 4, 7, 10..., every number is 3 more than the previous one. The number after 10 is 13. This is an arithmetic sequence. Everyone can do it.

Nadine faces a problem: find the pattern from the numbers in the table, and fill in the blanks.

Input (x)	6	8	11	5	7		
Output (y)	22	28			25	16	13

If we view it as a machine then the machine runs according to a certain rule. If we input 6, we get 22; if we input 8, the output is 28, etc. Then what is its rule? Dominic remembers the method taught by Dr.C: When the input changes from 6 to 7 then to 8, it increases by 1 each time; the corresponding output number changes 3 each time, from 22 to 25 to 28; therefore the first step is to multiply the input number by 3. However the work is not finished, multiply the number 6 by 3 the result is 18 not 22, so we should add 4 to it as the second step. The rule therefore is ×3, then +4. The table now becomes:

×3, +4

Input (x)	6	8	11	5	7	4	3
Output (y)	22	28	37	19	25	16	13

Here the first step is important: **When the input x increases or decreases by 1, the output changes correspondingly by a, then multiply the input by a first.**

Sarah's question is somewhat different. She is required to find the pattern in 361, 324, 289, 256, etc. Sarah is smart; she finds not only one, but two patterns for one question. Method one is to study the difference between adjacent numbers: $361 - 324 = 37$, $324 - 289 = 35$, $289 - 256 = 33$, hence the next difference should be 31 and the next number is $256 - 31 = 225$. Sarah's second pattern is even simpler. Because she remembers the squares of 1 to 30 very well, she realizes that the given numbers 361, 324, 289, 256 are just 19^2, 18^2, 17^2 and 16^2, the next number should be $15^2 = 225$.

Sometimes you are given with letters instead of numbers. For instance what should be the next alphabetical letter after h, l, and p? Dominic points out that the letter h is the 8th one in English alphabet, l is the 12th, and p is the 16th, so that the next should be the 20th (t). The rule is clear, skip three and choose the next English letter each time.

1.7 Rules of making turns

Dr.C asked the class: "To make a turn is simple, we do it many times a day. However, do you know the rules of making turns?"

"A GPS tells a driver to turn left or right, not to turn east or north. Let us use this left --- right way to study the rules of turns. Question 1: when you go from place A to place B, assume that you make a right turn (R); when you come back from B to A, should you turn left (L) or turn right (R)?"

"Easy!" students answered immediately. "Turn left!"

"Correct," said Dr.C. "When you reverse the path, R becomes L and L becomes R. Just make the turn the opposite way. That is simple.

"Now, question 2: When you go from A to B assume that you turn left first then turn right (i.e., LR) then when you come back from B to A, how do you make your turns, still LR, or change to RL?"

Some students said "LR", others answered "RL".

Dr.C smiled, drew a diagram on the white board. It became clear that "when you go, turn left first then turn right, when you come back, still turn left first then turn right". LR became LR!

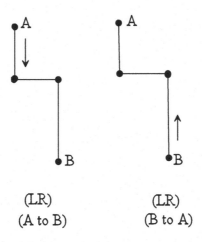

(LR)
(A to B)

(LR)
(B to A)

"Consider another situation: If when you go you make four turns RLRL, then when you come back you need to turn RLRL again."

Bruce and Linda complained: "Dear Dr. C, we are confused. The first example tells us, L becomes R, and R becomes L; when we come back we should make the turn the *opposite* way. However the second situation (4 turns, go RLRL, come back RLRL) seems to suggest us another story. When we come back the order should be the *same* as we go! Which way is correct?"

Dr.C said: "It is incorrect to claim that when you come back the order should be the same as you go. Just imagine, if you go by RRR, when you come back you should turn LLL (see the diagram), then you know the turns cannot be the same."

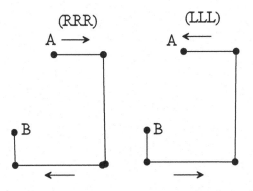

"Then how do we explain the question where LR still becomes LR? Let us study that diagram in more details.

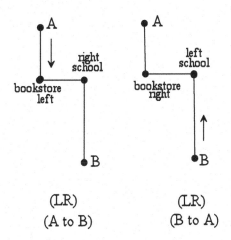

"You see, when you go from A to B, you make left turn at the bookstore then right turn at the school, when you come back from B to A you make left turn at the school, then right turn at the bookstore. So it is actually L(bookstore)R(school) to L(school)R(bookstore). At every turning point (e.g., at the bookstore) the direction is really changed! At the bookstore L becomes R, at the school R becomes L. When we go from A to B we arrive at the bookstore first, when we come back from B to A we arrive at the school first. Two changes (arriving order and direction of turn) make it seem as if it were 'not changed'.

17

"Now, question 3: If when you go you make 7 turns RLRLLRL, what should be the answer when you come back? "

Students did this as an exercise in class with great interest. The answer of course should be RLRRLRL.

1.8   Number games

Today young students Richard and Julia played the number game *Sudoku*, a popular game played all over the world (To play *Sudoku*, just input numbers 1 to 9 in smart ways so that each row, each column, and evry 3×3 grid have the numbers 1 to 9). After a while Julia said: "May I ask you a question?"

"Please," said Richard.

"Numbers are afraid of one of them, which one?"

"Oh, it is 7. Because when we say 7, 8, 9, it sounds like *seven ate nine*."

Richard also asked back Julia a question: "One day a fisherman caught 6 fish no head, 9 fish no tail, and 8 half-fish. How many did he catch on that day?"

Julia replied: "That fisherman caught nothing on that day. Because 6 without head is a 0, 9 without tail is a 0, and half of 8 is also a 0."

They continued to play with each other. Julia asked Richard: "Can you add just one line and change the wrong expression 1 + 5 +5 = 150 into a correct math equation?" [1]

Richard answered, and asked Julia a similar question: "Can you add just one line and change 10 10 10 to *nine fifty* ?" [2]

Julia then asked Richard: "Can you put 8 cats into 9 empty rooms so that no room is empty after that? Also, can you place 9 cats into 8 empty rooms such that no room has more than one cat?" [3]

Richard fought back: "Do you know, what is the longest word in English, and what is the shortest word (except "*I*") in English?" [4]

Answers to these funny questions can be found at the end of the chapter.

1.9   Easy ways to convert units

Alice and her younger sister Isabella study in different grades. One day they asked Dr.C whether there was an easy way to convert units.

Dr.C replied: "Yes. Units conversion is important. If you want to compare the speeds of four animals, and you know that A runs 180 cm distance in 1 second; B runs 110 m in 1 minute; C can run 3000 m in 1 hour; and D can run 15 km in one day, you need to convert units first then compare the speeds under the same units. In order to convert units we have different methods for different grade students. Isabella, you are young and you just began to study units. Let me tell you a method for beginners. Here is an example of distance, let me draw the following scaled line.

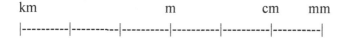

km   m   cm   mm
|---------|----------|----------|----------|----------|----------|

"To convert 56 m to km, follow the diagram you need to go left 3 steps from m to km. Therefore we move the decimal point to the left three places. 56 is 56.0, move the point three places to the left and we get 0.056 km. Now, can you tell me how many cm or mm is 7.1 m?"

Isabella followed Dr.C's example, from the diagram it was clear that to go from m to cm or mm, you had to go right 2 or 3 steps respectively. Hence Isabella's answers were:

$$7.1m = 710cm = 7100mm$$

This method could be applied to mass (mg, g, kg, t), volume (L, mL, etc.) or other quantities, just drew corresponding units lines.

Alice asked a more comprehensive question. "How can we convert a speed of 72 km/h to m/s?"

The method she learned from her school was:

$$72\frac{km}{h} = 72\frac{km}{hour} \times \frac{1000\,m}{1km} \times \frac{1\,hour}{60\,min} \times \frac{1\,min}{60\,sec} = 20\frac{m}{sec}$$

(It was complicated.)

"Well," said Dr.C. " There is a simpler way. Why not view 72 km/h as 'a number *times* a unit', that is,

$$72\frac{km}{h} = 72 \times \frac{1km}{1hour}$$

"Now since $1km = 1000m$ and $1h = 60\min = 3600\sec$, we replace the units as

$$72\frac{km}{h} = 72 \times \frac{1km}{1h} = 72 \times \frac{1000m}{3600s} = \left(72 \times \frac{1000}{3600}\right)\frac{m}{s}$$

"**Note the brackets at the last step.** Whatever complicated math inside the brackets, the outside units are already the units you want. So, ignore the units, just evaluate the math *inside* the brackets and the work is done."

"More than that, we know 1 m = 100 cm, but what can we do if we want to know, say, how many cm^3 is $0.042m^3$?"

Dr.C explained: "Just cube both sides (to calculate areas, just square both sides) and we get

$$1m = 100cm$$
$$(1m)^3 = (100cm)^3$$
$$1m^3 = 1000000cm^3$$

Therefore $0.042m^3 = 0.042 \times 1000000cm^3 = 42000cm^3$

Next, Dr.C said: "In the USA, temperature is measured in Fahrenheit. In Canada temperature is measured in Celsius. To convert $°C$ to$°F$, multiply the temperature T by 9 then divide the answer by 5, then add 32. To convert $°F$ into $°C$, first subtract 32 degrees from the given temperature, then multiply the answer by 5 and divide it by 9. Thus a typical human body temperature $37°C$ would be close to $100°F$.

"Now let me tell you a story. On a Christmas Day, American girl Jessica came to Canada to visit her cousin Danny. In Danny's house Jessica asked Danny what was the temperature outside. They found that the degree in Fahrenheit happened to be the same as the degree Celsius. Do you know what that day's temperature outside Danny's house was?" (The answer is at the end of the chapter).

1.10 Secret of multiplication

Multiplication has a secret, many people do multiplication many times everyday but do not realize it. Today, Dr.C wrote $57 \times 68 = 3876$ on the board.

"5 plus 7 is 12; go on to do $1 + 2 = 3$. 6 plus 8 is 14, then add the two digits 1 and 4 the answer is 5," said Dr.C. "Now the left side becomes 3×5, which yields 15. Continue to squeeze the digits we have $1 + 5 = 6$."

"What is the right side? $3 + 8 + 7 + 6 = 24$, $2 + 4 = 6$. Both sides got the same number!"

"Is this a coincidence? No. All multiplications satisfy the same rule. For example $6749 \times 4587 = 30957663$. The left side $6 + 7 + 4 + 9 = 26 \rightarrow 8$ and $4 + 5 + 8 + 7 = 24 \rightarrow 6$; continue to squeeze and we get $8 \times 6 = 48 \rightarrow 4 + 8 = 12 \rightarrow 1 + 2 = 3$. Do the same thing to the

22

right side, we get $3+0+9+5+7+6+6+3 = 39 \rightarrow 12 \rightarrow 3$ (the same number)."

Dr.C continued: "This property can be used to check whether a multiplication question is done correctly or to find a missing number. If the above question is written as $6749 \times 4587 = 3095?663$ with an unknown digit (the ?), squeeze the right side we get $32+? \rightarrow 5+?$, while the left side result is unchanged (3). Therefore $5+? \rightarrow 3$, the answer can only be 7 (that is, $5+7 = 12 \rightarrow 3$)."

"To prove this property exceeds the plan of this lesson, however it is easy to use many examples to verify it," says Dr.C. "If the unknown number is a 0 or 9, be careful! We should realize that there are two possibilities. For instance 203 yields 2+0+3=5, while 293 yields $2+9+3 = 14 \rightarrow 5$, same result. In order to get 5 the question mark in $2?3$ could be 0 and could also be 9. If the missing number is 1 to 8 then there is no ambiguity, the result is unique."

1.11 Math magic to surprise the audience

Yesterday evening Dr.C and his students held a party. During the party many good shows came on one after another. When it was Dr.C's turn he smiled and told the audience: "Let me present a math magic show for everyone. We all know that among the four operations (addition, subtraction, multiplication and division) division is the most difficult one. Now let me show you how to do a division without a pen, without a calculator or even a piece of paper --- just use my brain."

"However," said Dr.C "if we do not apply any restrictions the quotient obtained from a division may contain many decimals. For instance a simple division $16 \div 17$ produces $0.94117647058823529\ldots$. How can we avoid such a trouble? The following way can guarantee that the answer of a division must be a whole number. Please think of a 2 digit number (like 19, 78, or any other), keep it in secret and do not tell me. Now please multiply your secret number by 10 and tell me the result. I will divide your answer by 10 in my brain, and find out what was your original number. Say, if your result is 120 then I know your secret number must be 12, because $120 \div 10 = 12$. I do that division in my head without a calculator."

"That's not hard, we can do it!" said many students.

"Well, this is too easy," smiled Dr.C. "Let me do a harder one. Please multiply your secret 2 digit number by a number greater than 10. Can you tell me a greater number?"

"84" said Felix.

"Still too small" said Dr.C with a laugh.

"How about 9348?" asked Elizabeth.

"Still not challenging enough," said Dr.C. "Let us make the number even greater. This way, let us use 934889. Use your calculator, multiply your 2 digit number by this big number and tell me your result. I will divide your answer by 934889 in my head."

Everyone was astonished. They looked at each other. No one believed that Dr.C could do such a long division in head without using a calculator or a pen. Helen used the number 69; she used her calculator and found that $934889 \times 69 = 64507341$. Just after she reported her answer 64507341, Dr.C immediately said: "Your number must be 69."

The answer of Eugene was 54223562, Dr.C immediately pointed out that the original number of Eugene was 58. The whole class was surprised! Even if you used a calculator to evaluate $54223562 \div 934889$, you still needed to press the buttons 16 times. How could Dr.C do that division so fast!

More students tried, all of them were surprised. What was the secret?

Oh, Dr.C's secret was as following: "When people tell you the answer, **ignore all the digits except the last two, multiply those 2 digits by 9 in your head and report the last two digits of the product.**"

For example when Helen told Dr.C that her answer was 64507341, do not listen to all but the last two digits 41. Then use your brain to multiply 41 by 9, which is not difficult. Because $41 \times 9 = 369$, her original 2 digit number was just the last 2 digits here: 69. For Eugene, his answer was 54223562. Again just remember the last 2 digits 62 and ignore all others. $62 \times 9 = 558$ so his original secret number was 58. So simple! Dr.C was not mentally calculating $54223562 \div 934889$, instead he only calculated 62×9, it was much easier!

Today Dr.C further revealed the secret: "In order to make it working, that 934889 **must end with 89**. Other digits (9348) are irrelevant at all; you can ask the audience to choose randomly. To use 4876589 or 77294089 makes no difference." Since 9348 was chosen by the students (not by Dr.C), the effect was quite amazing.

The math truth behind the magic show is that since $89 \times 9 = 801$, and any two digit number multiplied by 801 the result ends with the same two digits. Examples: $17 \times 801 = 13617$ (ended with 17), $48 \times 801 = 38448$ (ended with 48), $96 \times 801 = 76896$ (ended with 96), etc.

Dr.C said: "If the audience ever suspects that the number added by me (89) might have a problem, then I would discard it immediately and change it to 67 (pretend to make the change randomly). This time multiply the last 2 digits of the product by 3 (not 9), and the magic show still holds! The audience would be even more surprised!" (Example: in Eugene's case $58 \times 934867 = 54222286$, $86 \times 3 = 258$, ended with 58).

1.12 Infinite possibilities

Today's class was especially interesting. Dr.C first asked the students to write the English spelling for numbers 0, 1, 2, 3, (i.e., zero, one, two, three), then asked them: "Among these four words, does any one follow the order of letters in the English alphabet?"

Soon the students found that not one of these four words followed the English alphabet (Letter *a* should be before all other letters, *b* should be behind *a* but in front of all other letters, etc). (*Zero* started with *z*, *One* put *n* before *e*, similarly for *two* and *three*).

Dr.C then encouraged the students to continue the test, trying 4, 5, 6, and any other numbers. Dr.C said: "You may consider *any* huge number, fraction, decimal, negative number regardless of how large or how small it is. I can tell you, in the whole world there is *only one* number whose spelling follows the English alphabet.

"The difficulty is, we are unable to try all the numbers in the universe. There are *infinitely* manly numbers. Even if you already tried a thousand times, you still don't know what might happen to the next number.

How can we be sure that there is no second number which satisfies the requirement?" (The answer is at the end of the chapter).

After a discussion Dr.C raised another question: "On various books you can find a question similar to the following one. A store sells boxes of cakes. One large box contains 18 cakes, one mid-size box contains 12 cakes, and one small box contains 5 cakes. You are not allowed to open the box and sell part of it. If you want 22 cakes, you may buy 2 small boxes plus one medium box. If you want 6 or 13 cakes it is simply impossible. What is the *maximum impossible* number of cakes (the number that you cannot buy)? Please notice, this is a theoretical question so even thousands or millions of cakes are allowed. The difficulty here is that again there are infinite numbers. Even if you find a way to make 16487 cakes, how do you know that 16488, 16499, etc are possible or not possible? We cannot just try numbers one after another endlessly. This is a problem of infinite possibilities."

Dr.C said: "Although this question was not invented by me, but my method to solve it is somewhat special. I draw a bag and write whole numbers 1 to 18 into it. I call 'possible to provide' numbers as 'good numbers', and those impossible to provide as 'bad numbers'. Now, please find all good numbers in the first bag.

"In the first bag there are 18 numbers (1 to 18). Only 5, 10, 12, 15, 17, and 18 are 'good numbers' (in the diagram shown as numbers without brackets). For example, $10 = 2 \times 5$, two small size boxes make 10 so 10 is a good number   In the same diagram I use brackets for bad numbers, for example (4) is a bad number.

"Now, listen carefully: Please add every 'bad number' in the bag by 18, write the answer into the *next* bag. Here is an **important rule**: if a number is already a good number, do not write the result into the next bag. Why not? Because any good number plus 18 must still be a good number .

27

For example 17 is good (17 = 12 + 5, one medium box plus one small box), so 17+18 = 35 *must be* good (one medium box plus one small box plus one large box). Due to this reason we do not need to try any good number plus 18. Thus, the second bag contains less numbers than the first bag, and so on."

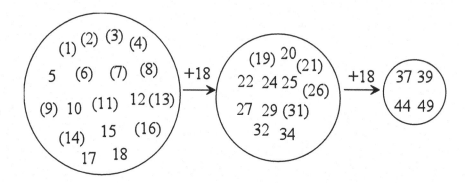

Dr.C continued: "In the first bag there are six good numbers (5, 10, 12, 15, 17, and 18). These numbers will not proceed to the second bag. So the second bag has only 12 numbers ($18 - 6 = 12$). Among them eight numbers 20, 22, 24, 25, 27, 29, 32 and 34 are new good numbers. (Please try each by yourself). Now add the four bad numbers by 18 and make the third bag. The third bag only has four numbers in it: 37, 39, 44 and 49.

"All the four numbers in the third bag are good numbers, possible to make. As an example $37 = 5 \times 5 + 12$ (5 small bags plus one medium bag). The result is, all four numbers in the third bag are possible. There is no need to go on the process since any good number plus 18 is still a good number. It is now clear that the maximum bad number is 31 in the second box. Using only three bags and we found the answer. This smart method changes an infinite problem to a limited case problem. Isn't it impressive?"

Finally Dr.C said :"When we face infinite possibilities, we should not just try one by one, we should not trust an answer obtained from only limited number of trials. Even if you tried 100 times and every time you were successful, you still cannot guarantee that the 101st trial will be successful. The expression $\dfrac{1}{43-k}$ is less than 1 for k values from 0, 1, 2, to 41, and also correct for k values 44, 45,... However it is not less than 1 if $k = 42$ (it equals 1 if $k = 42$). Even if you have proved $\dfrac{1}{43-k} < 1$ forty one times, it is still wrong for the next value of $k = 42$. To prove math conclusions for infinite cases there is a special method called 'mathematical induction'. That method is useful and you will study it in your future school years, so I won't talk about it today in this class."

Answers:

Section 1.3
"Simple is beautiful"

Section 1.8
[1] Change the equal sign = to ≠, or (better) add one stroke to the plus sign so that "+" becomes "4", 145+5=150.

[2] On the top of the middle 10, add a line and change it to T, so that "10 10 10" becomes "10 To 10". (when we talk about time, "10 to 10" means time 9:50).

[3]

E	I	G	H	T	C	A	T	S

N	I	N	E	C	A	T	S

[4] The long word is "*smiles*", from the fist letter to the last you pass a '*mile*'. The shortest word is *envelope*, one envelope usually has only one *letter* in it.

Section 1.9
$-40°C = -40°F$.

Section 1.12
Forty (40). Why?

Chapter 2
Perimeter and Area

2.1   Side lengths and internal angles of a triangle

Triangles are fundamental in geometry. The   sum   of   the   three internal angles $\angle A + \angle B + \angle C$ is $180°$. If there are two obtuse angles, the two sides would not be able to meet each other on a plane. There is no similar restriction to the three sides. The restriction to the sides a, b, and c is only relative: the sum of any two must be longer than the third one. As to the absolute values of the side length, there is no restriction. The length can be in order of millimeters, centimeters, meters, kilometers or even longer. The perimeter of a triangle can be as small as the diameter of a pin hole, or as larger as the size of a country. Ironically, the only restriction to the sides does not apply to the angles either; an internal angle of a triangle can easily be greater than the sum of the other two angles. A triangle of internal angles $178°$, $1°$ and $1°$ is completely possible, whereas a triangle of side lengths 178 cm, 1 cm and 1cm is simply impossible. Angles do not follow the restriction of sides; sides do not obey the requirement of angles. The rules are fair.

Dr.C asked his students to provide some examples of triangles seen in everyday life. After that he said: "Although in any triangle the largest angle must be opposite to the longest side, the smallest angle must be opposite to the shortest side, there is no proportional relation between sides and angles. If one angle is twice as big as another, the corresponding side lengths do not satisfy the 2 to 1 ratio. Just look at the example mentioned above, while a triangle of $178°$, $1°$, $1°$ is reasonable, its side lengths cannot be $178:1:1$; instead, the sides satisfy $1.9997:1:1$.

"We are familiar with right triangles. If C is the vertex of a right angle, we have $\angle A + \angle B = \angle C$ and $a^2 + b^2 = c^2$ but not $a + b = c$. The relations between angles and sides are the sine law and the cosine law in trigonometry, which you will learn later.

"When one internal angle of a triangle is fixed, if another angle is increasing, the third one must be decreasing. There is no similar relation among the sides. All three sides can increase or decrease at the same time, as long as they obey the requirement that the sum of any two be longer than the third one. There is no rule such as 'if you grow up I must shrink down size'."

"As to other shapes," said Dr.C, "the sum of the four internal angles of any quadrilateral is $360°$, and the sum of the four sides can be as large or as short as you want. You may further study quadrilaterals, pentagons, hexagons, etc., by yourself".

2.2 *P* and *A* apparently impossible to find

"Sometimes the conditions given in a problem seem to be not enough to solve the problem. However actually it could be possible. We may be able to find the answer from the given conditions". Dr.C drew a diagram on the board and continued: "A student ran one lap around her school, the map of her school is shown here. How many meters did she run?"

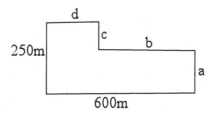

"The mystery part of this question is that, in the diagram we only know the length of two sides, not the four unknown sides *a*, *b*, *c* and *d*. We should not assume that the diagram was drawn to scale. **Anything not given by a problem should not be assumed to be true.**

"Wow! This problem is actually good, because we do not need to know these four sides. Although we do not know *a*, *b*, *c* and *d*, we do know $a + c = 250$ m and $b + d = 600$ m for sure. Thus the perimeter can be calculated as $250 + 600 + (a + c) + (d + d) = 1700$ m. This has nothing to do with the details of each section (like how long *a* is). The fact that the diagram bends here or there does not affect the result.

"Please imagine that you are Gulliver travelling in a tiny kingdom, pushing the two sides out until the shape becomes a rectangle. Because the sides do not change while you push them, the perimeter of the rectangle is the same as the perimeter of the original figure --- only easier to evaluate.

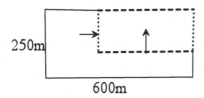

"If the shape has concave parts like the one in the following diagram (left), in order to calculate the perimeter we do not need to know the length of *a*, but we need to know the length of *b*. Because when we push the side *a* out to get a rectangle (the right side figure), the two sides *b* still exist.

33

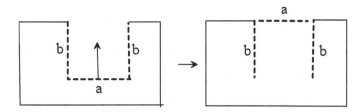

"Does an area have the similar situation that 'apparently impossible to calculate, but actually possible'? Yes, please see the following diagram:

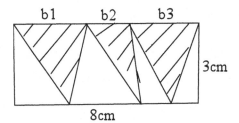

"Without knowing the details (b_1, b_2, b_3), it seems to be impossible to find the total area of the shaded regions in the diagram. However,

$$\Delta_1 + \Delta_2 + \Delta_3 = \tfrac{1}{2} \times b_1 \times 3 + \tfrac{1}{2} \times b_2 \times 3 + \tfrac{1}{2} \times b_3 \times 3$$
$$= \tfrac{1}{2}(b_1 + b_2 + b_3) \times 3 = \tfrac{1}{2} \times 8 \times 3 = 12cm^2$$

"We do not need to know how the 8 cm side is divided into 3 segments. Even if the 8 cm side is divided into more segments, we still do not need to know the details. The total area of the shaded regions is exactly half of the original rectangle."

Through this lesson the students learned more about the perimeter and the area of geometric figures, they completed a "mission impossible".

2.3 Why not raise questions in the opposite way?

If the perimeter of a quadrilateral is fixed, what shape will have the maximum area? If the area of a quadrilateral is fixed, what shape will produce the minimum perimeter?

These questions are simple. The answers are the same: when the quadrilateral is a square. We can prove it with high school math, such proofs can be found in many textbooks. If the students are not yet in high school, it can be verified by comparing rectangles like 0.5×5.5, 1×5, 2×4, 3×3 etc. Among these rectangles of perimeter 12 units, the square (3×3) has the greatest area.

Today Dr.C did not stop there. He said: "Let us consider the situation further. Can we raise the questions in the opposite direction? If the perimeter of a rectangle is given, under what situation is its area the *minimum*? If the area of a rectangle is fixed, under what situation is its perimeter the *maximum*?"

Students discussed these new questions. Most students thought it might not be proper to ask questions in that way. Dr. C said: "You are right, we don't ask questions in the opposite way, but *why not*? Simply because these questions do not have an answer! The result has no limit. 'Maximum perimeter' and 'minimum area' simply do not exist.

"Use the rectangle of perimeter 12 cm as an example, if it is 1×5, its area is 5 cm^2; if it is 0.5×5.5, its area is 2.75 cm^2; if it is 0.01×5.99, its area becomes 0.0599 cm^2. Obviously the area could be even smaller, could be as small as you want."

Dr.C then asked the class: "Is it possible that the perimeter of a rectangle is very large, say, 1000 km (longer than the size of many countries), but its area is just 1 or 2 m^2 (as small as my desk)? Also, is it possible that a rectangle with an area as small as a nail has a perimeter longer than 1 km, 10 km, 100 km or even more?"

The whole class was surprised. Oh, math questions could be asked that way! We never saw such a question in our textbooks. Problems found in our textbooks were usually normal, in order of cm, m, and km. Dr.C said: "The truth is that, the above questions are indeed possible! If an extremely slim rectangle has a length of 500 km and the width is only 1/500 of one mm, then the perimeter of that rectangle is 1000 km and the area is only 1 m^2. It requires a little bit imagination but it is possible. On the other hand, in order to get a rectangle of area 1 cm^2 and perimeter 10 km, we just need the length and width to be 5 km and 0.000002 cm respectively.

"In these two cases we have 'very small area, very large perimeter'. Can we switch the two concepts and ask a question of 'very small perimeter, very large area'? Such a situation however is ridiculous. It is impossible to enclose a big area by a small length perimeter. In order to enclose a rectangular area 100 m^2 by bending a straight line, at least we need 40 m perimeter (to get a square of side length 10 m). If the rectangle is not a square we need even more than that."

Dr.C guided the discussion further. He pointed out: "The reason to have these situations is due to the fundamental difference between addition and multiplication. 'Small area, large perimeter' is possible, whereas 'large area , small perimeter' is impossible. This is because we calculate the perimeter by addition, and calculate the area by multiplication. Adding 100 to 0.0001, the result is still (almost) 100, multiplying 100 by 0.0001 the answer suddenly reduces to 0.01. When we add two numbers, the bigger one dominates. When we multiply two numbers, the smaller one may be more important. Increase the number 100 by 0.0001 or by 0.00001, the results are almost identical. Whereas multiplying 100 by 0.0001, the answer is 10 times as large as the result of multiplying 100 by 0.00001, plus that the results are much smaller than the original number 100. Therefore the fact is that, to enclose an area, if the total length (perimeter) is too small the job cannot be done, if the total length is large or very large, it is possible."

In this lesson Dr.C used a method called "**pushing things to an extreme**". Such a method is useful in both math and physics. Through this lesson the students widely expanded their ways of thinking, learned something more thoroughly than what they usually do in schools. Teachers also admired: "Oh, a math lesson could be taught in such an impressive way!".

2.4 What happens if *P* and *A* have the same number?

Can the perimeter *P* and the area *A* of a figure equal to each other? No, never. They have different units and different meanings. However in order to encourage the kids to think more, today Dr.C asked the following question: "If we only check the numbers, not the units or meanings, what kind of square happens to have the same *number* in perimeter and area?"

Soon the students found the answer: a square of side length 4 units (perimeter 16 units and area 16 square units).

Dr.C smiled. "What if it's a rectangle, whose length is different from the width?"

This problem took longer to solve. Doug got one answer, it was a rectangle of 3×6 with a perimeter 18 and an area 18.

"I got another," claimed Clare. "My answer is a rectangle of length 2.5 and width 10. Its perimeter is 25, its area is also 25 with different units."

Selene and Jamie also found their own answers. Jamie's rectangle was 2.4 by 12, Selene's answer was 4.5 by 3.6. Simple calculations showed that both of them were right. Soon other students in the class found their different answers too.

"Excellent!" said Dr.C. "You see, there is only one answer for a square, while there exist many answers for a rectangle."

"We have learned more geometric shapes. Let us extend our question to more complicated cases. If the perimeter and the area of an equilateral triangle happen to be the same *in number*, what is the side length of it?

"Assume that the side length is x, its perimeter is $3x$. From the Pythagorean Theorem we know that its altitude is $h = \dfrac{\sqrt{3}}{2}x$. Therefore when $x = 4\sqrt{3}$, both the perimeter and the area ($\dfrac{1}{2}hx$) have the same number $12\sqrt{3}$.

"Next, let us study a circle. What is the size of a circle with the same number of circumference and area?"

Soon the answer was found, it was a circle of radius 2. Such a circle had a circumference 4π and an area 4π.

Dr.C did not stop, he asked the class more questions:

"[1]　What is the side length of a cube with the same number in volume and total surface area?

"[2]　If the total length of all edges of a cube happens to be the same as the volume of the cube, what is the length of one side?

"[3]　If the surface area of a sphere equals the volume in number, what is the radius of the sphere?

"[4]　The total surface area of a cylinder happens to be the same as the volume of that cylinder, what are the height and the radius? What is the relation between h and r ?"

The class got surprised. Because the answers of question [4] were exactly the same as the rectangle question asked above (when area "equals" perimeter in number). You might think that there was no relation between a rectangle (2-D, formed by straight line segments) and a cylinder (3-D, containing curves). However, the truth was surprising. All answers of one problem were exactly the same as the answers of the other problem. For instance, in Selene's answer (a rectangle of dimension 3.6 by 4.5) its perimeter "equals" its area in number. A cylinder of radius 3.6 and height 4.5 (or radius 4.5, height 3.6) also had a similar property: its total surface area "equals" its volume in number. Readers are encouraged to calculate and prove that in general. Of course answers found above by Clare (2.5×10), Jamie (2.4×12), Doug (3×6) or other students *all* satisfied that relation. You might switch the two dimensions (e.g., a cylinder of radius 3, height 6; or a cylinder of radius 6 and height 3) and you would still find that each combination satisfied the same requirement!

Dear readers, can you prove this property in general?

2.5   The most cost-effective fence

Today is a fine day. Dr.C invited his friend Mr. Martin to the classroom to observe a math lesson. At the classroom Dr.C introduced Mr. Martin to the class and said: "My friends, Mr. Martin is a successful farmer. One of the things Mr. Martin needs to do is building a fence around his field. Do you know, there are lots of math in building a fence?"

Dr.C asked the class: "Can we use only 1 m long fence to enclose a region of area 10000 m^2 ?"

"No!" answered the students without hesitation.

Dr.C then asked the next question: "If Mr. Martin already has a fence around a rectangular lot, can he add just 1 m fence to enclose 10000 m^2 more area?"

Various answers emerged from the students. Some agreed, others disagreed. Tom said: "How can we dream such a wonderful thing? Assume that 1 m fence costs 1 dollar, then how can we expect to spend only $1 more, one can enclose an area larger than our school? This can only exist in the story of *Arabian Nights*."

Even Mr. Martin was surprised: "That is too wonderful to be true! I never dared to imagine such a good thing."

Tina pointed out: "However, what Dr.C said was '1 m longer', not '1 m long'. Also he only asked about the *increase* of an area."

"Correct," said Dr.C. "Please pay attention to the word '*more*'. Assume that Mr. Martin's field is 20000 m long and 100 m wide, if the width changes to 100.5 m, the effect on the change of perimeter is negligible, only add 1 m (or **0.0025%**). However, the area now increases from 2000000 m^2 to 2010000 m^2, increased by 10000 m^2. Isn't that a good news? A small increase of the width (0.5 m only) brings a big increase to the area (an increase of 10000 m^2). Obviously it would not be hard if you want to increase the area by 50000 m^2 or 100000 m^2.

"It is important to know that, in this example the width 100 m is not important at all. If the width is 1 m or 10 m instead of 100 m, the results are still the same. In order to increase the area by 10000 m^2 you only need to add the width by 0.5 m regardless of how much the original width is. (Example: 20000 ×1 becomes 20000 ×1.5, the area increases by 10000 m^2). How long the width is does not affect the answer, as long as the *other* side is long.

"Suppose that Mr. Martin spends the same amount of money to increase the long side (the *length*) by 0.5 m for a 20000 m long 1 m wide rectangular lot, that is, to change 20000 ×1 into 20000.5 ×1, the effect would be quite different. The perimeter still increases by 1 m, but the area this time only increases by 0.5 m^2. What a big difference! Spending the same amount of money only results a much smaller amount of increase of area."

Finally Dr.C told the students: "The lesson is, in order to increase the area of a rectangle, we should avoid increasing the longer side, instead we are better off spending the same money to increase the shorter side --- this way is far more effective.

"Well, let me explain this in more details. Compare $m+n+1$ with $m+n$, the results increases by 1 regardless of the fact whether m is increased or n is increased. Compare mn to $m(n+1)$, the answer is increased by m. You change n to $(n+1)$, the effect is to increase the product *mn* by *m*. If the unchanged number *m* is large enough, a little change of *n* may cause a large change in the product. So in multiplication (unlike addition) we change *n* and get a result decided by *m*, we say 'pay attention to the other number in multiplication'.

"To a rectangle of dimension 10000×1, an increase of the length 10000 by 1 means a relative change of the length by only 1/10000; while an increase of 1 on the width (to change the width from 1 to 2) means a 100% change. Spending money to increase the shorter side is more efficient."

Dr.C's students studied this lesson with great enthusiasm. Mr. Martin the farmer also praised the lesson: "I see, there are so many math truths on the topic of fences."

2.6 Finding an area from the side lengths

If all side lengths of a closed geometric figure are given, can we find its area? Dr.C said: "That depends on the problem."

[Triangles]

For any triangle if we know all three sides, we know everything of it, including the three internal angles (the shape of the triangle), the area, the three medians, the three altitudes. All these are fixed and can be calculated. If the three sides of a triangle are a, b, and c, the area of the triangle is

$A = \sqrt{s(s-a)(s-b)(s-c)}$, where $s = \frac{1}{2}(a+b+c)$ is half of the perimeter

(the Heron Theorem). Junior grade students have not learned the cosine law of trigonometry so they cannot derive the Heron Theorem. Instead, the teacher may use examples to *verify* it. For example a right triangle of base 3 and height 4, has an area 6 square units. Using Heron Theorem ($P = 3 + 4 + 5 = 12$, $s = 6$) we get the same answer.

Contrary to this, if all three internal angles are known, the size of the triangle is not fixed, it can be larger or smaller, and there exist infinite number of similar triangles.

[Quadrilaterals]

If we know the perimeter of a square or the length and the width of a rectangle, we know its area. If we only know the perimeter of a rectangle, its area is uncertain.

A parallelogram is more complicated. Even if we already know the length of *every* side, the shape and area are still uncertain. In the diagram below we fix the bottom of a parallelogram and slide the top side parallel to the bottom. The altitude is changed and the area is changed ($A = bh$, the unchanged base b times the changed height h), but the perimeter remains the same.

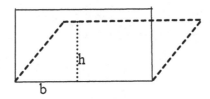

[Regular polygon, circle]

A circle has the most regular shape. If the circumference of a circle is fixed, the circle and its area are fixed. Similar situation happens for regular polygons. The following diagram shows a regular pentagon of side length a. The angle $\angle DOB = 36°$, the line segment DB is $\frac{1}{2}a$. The altitude

of triangle OAB is $OD = \dfrac{a}{2\tan 36°} = 0.688a$, hence the area of that triangle

can be calculated. Multiply the result by 5 we get the total area of the pentagon, therefore if we know the sides we know the area.

$$A = 5\triangle OAB = 5 \times \tfrac{1}{2} \times OD \times AB = 5 \times \tfrac{1}{2} \times 0.688a \times a = 1.72a^2$$

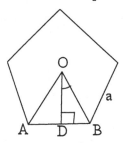

[Non-regular polygons]

What's about a non-regular, convex polygon? Could we still find its area just from the information about the length of every side? Students debated about this question. Some thought that for a n-side polygon if n was an odd number (like 5, 7, etc), then the conclusion obtained from a triangle $(n = 3)$ would be still applicable. Others disagreed.

Dr.C said: "It is not hard to find the answer. Just make a small change to the above diagram of a parallelogram, making it a non-regular 5-side polygon as shown in the following diagram.

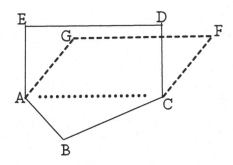

"The bottom part of the pentagon ABCDE is fixed, and the top part (CDEA) can slide. When the top DE slides, the length of every side is unchanged but the top area (hence the total area) is changed due to the slide. Therefore even if we already know all five sides, the shape of a non-regular pentagon is still changeable. Similar situation happens to polygons with $n > 5$. The conclusion: the area of a non-regular polygon ($n > 3$) is not fixed even if the lengths of all sides are known.

"From today's lesson we see that triangles are truly special. For any arbitrary shape triangle if we know all three sides, we know everything except the orientation of it."

2.7   Extra information, erroneous questions

Dr.C has several friends who teach math in schools. One day they had a party. Talking about the errors found in textbooks, Mr. Becker spoke first: "We know that textbooks have been proofread thoroughly, but still there exist errors in published textbooks, including printing errors (typos) in the text and mistakes at the answer key of the problems."

"Well, some errors are more serious. They are not accidental typos but theoretical mistakes," said Mrs. Myers. "I remember a textbook said:

'One side of a triangle is 6 cm shorter than another side, the third side is 3 times as long as the first one. The perimeter of this triangle is 206 cm, find all three sides of it. The intention of the author was to teach the students to learn how to solve coupled equations. However, if we really solve these equations we will get the following answers: 40cm, 46cm, and 120cm. Such three sides are unable to form a triangle. This is *not* a typo. This question is correct in algebra but wrong in geometry."

Mr. James added: "Another textbook problem states that we want to make 100 kg mixed candy from candy A ($40/kg) and candy B ($25/kg). The mixed candy should have a unit price of $21/kg. How many of each type candy should be used? Such a problem cannot have a meaningful answer since the price of the mixture must lie between the high and the low prices. The equations $\begin{cases} x + y = 100 \\ 40x + 25y = 21 \times 100 \end{cases}$ lead to one answer negative and the other more than 100 kg."

Ms. Singe said: "I have seen a problem in a textbook, which had no error in mathematics, but it was wrong in physics and astronomy. Let me describe the problem for you: 'Two satellites fly around the Earth in circular orbits. The orbit of one satellite is $x^2 + y^2 = 2250000 \; km^2$, the other ...'. The given equation does not look wrong, but it implies that the radius of the circular orbit around the Earth is $\sqrt{2250000} = 1500$ km. The radius of the Earth is 6380 km, how can the radius of the orbit be less than that? That means the satellite flies *inside* the solid Earth. Although there is no math mistake, the given equation is not acceptable. Maybe the author only knew math, did not know physics and astronomy"

Fellow teachers praised Ms. Singe for providing a good example. Mrs. Johnson showed another problem with hidden mistakes: "In a textbook there was a diagram like the one below. Find the area and perimeter of the given triangle (P=7+9+13=29 *cm* and A=$\frac{1}{2}$×6×13 = 39 *cm²*). However, we can calculate the length of the two sections of the base by Pythagorean Theorem and find that the base BC actually is BD + DC = $\sqrt{13} + \sqrt{45}$ = 10.3cm. Therefore such a problem is not self-consistent."

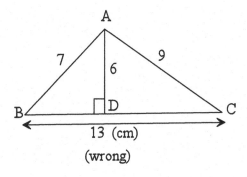

(wrong)

Mr. Dickens also laughed: "Hi, let me show all of you an example in another textbook. The problem has a diagram as below. Let us not point out the mistakes, instead, leave it as homework for our students to find the error. It would be a good training."

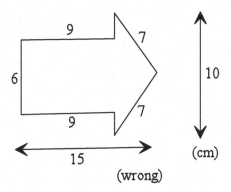

(wrong)

This is the diagram shown by Mr. Dickens during that party. Caution: errors in this problem are hidden, not obvious.

Chapter 3
Fractions, Decimals, Factors

3.1   Surprises when comparing fractions

In a math class at Dr.C Learning Center, Dr.C asked the students: "What are the ways to know whether a fraction is greater than, equal to, or less than another fraction?" Students spoke one after another. Helen said: "If two fractions have the same denominator then the one with a greater numerator is greater. If two fractions have the same numerator then the one with a smaller denominator is greater". Lisa said that if two fractions have different denominators we can change them into the same denominator first. Peter suggested to convert each fraction into a decimal then it is simple to decide which one is larger.

Dr.C agreed that all those methods were applicable, then he told the class a story: 38 students from the Apollo School competed in math against 39 students from the Fox School. The contest was difficult and only some of the students passed the contest. The results were:

Grade 5: 7 of the 12 students from the Apollo School passed the test. 4 of the 7 students from the Fox School passed the test.

Grade 6: 5 of the 8 students from the Apollo School passed the test. 4 of the 7 students from the Fox School passed the test.

Grade 7: 14 of the 18 students from the Apollo School passed the test. 19 of the 25 students from the Fox School passed the test.

Please calculate which school should win the contest.

[Grade 5]

Apollo $\dfrac{7}{12}$ passed, Fox $\dfrac{4}{7}$ passed, which school did better?

Conclusion: The Apollo won, because $\dfrac{7}{12} = 0.58$, and $\dfrac{4}{7} = 0.57$.

Another way was to convert the fractions into the same denominator: $\dfrac{7}{12} = \dfrac{49}{84}$, $\dfrac{4}{7} = \dfrac{48}{84}$

[Grade 6]

Apollo $\dfrac{5}{8} = 0.63$ passed, Fox $\dfrac{4}{7} = 0.57$ same as before. The Apollo won again.

[Grade 7]

Apollo $\dfrac{14}{18} = 0.78$ passed, Fox $\dfrac{19}{25} = 0.76$ passed, The Apollo won again.

There were only three grades in that contest, among them the Apollo won in *every* grade. The students of the Apollo School felt happy, although they just won a small margin over the opponent. However, at the closing ceremony Mrs. Smith, the referee, claimed that the Fox School won the contest and received the big trophy. All students from the Apollo School felt not fair. Did Mrs. Smith make a mistake?

Mrs. Smith explained: "We awarded the winning trophy to the Fox School because overall they did better."

"How could that be true?" complained the Apollo students. "There are only three grades in this contest. We won the test in every grade. Of course we won the whole contest!"

Mrs. Smith replied: "Well, girls and boys, let us compare the scores of your schools. The Apollo School sent $12 + 8 + 18 = 38$ students to the contest and $7 + 5 + 14 = 26$ of them passed. The Fox School sent $7 + 7 + 25 = 39$ students to the contest and $4 + 4 + 19 = 27$ of them passed."

The fractions of the students who passed the contest were:

The Apollo School: $\dfrac{26}{38} = 0.68 = 68\%$

The Fox School: $\dfrac{27}{39} = 0.69 = 69\%$.

So the miracle happened! The Fox who lost every test won the overall contest. The Apollo who did better in every grade lost the contest overall. The winning trophy should really be awarded to the Fox School! Three smaller trophies representing each grade should be awarded to the Apollo School team. Something "impossible" did happen!

Every student learned a math lesson from Dr.C's story. At the end of the class Dr.C said smiling: "Nevertheless, if in each grade the Apollo did win a lot, not just over a small margin, then the conclusion was obvious --- the Apollo won overall. In that case there was really no need for any calculation!"

3.2   Exploring fractions

Jenny and friends are learning fractions in school these days. Today Jenny invited Dr.C and several higher grade students to join a discussion. They talked about the mistakes they made and discussed the ways to avoid those mistakes.

Jenny said first: "I used to simplify fractions in a wrong way --- just simplify part of them. For instance I used to simplify $\dfrac{8+12}{4}$ as $\dfrac{4+12}{2}$. That is wrong since these two expressions one equals 5 and the other equals 8. It should be done as $\dfrac{8+12}{4} = \dfrac{4+6}{2} = 5$."

Yesinia, a higher grade student, said: "Such an error could come even in high school math. For example we may partially simplify a rational expression $\dfrac{6x^4-5}{4x^3}$ as $\dfrac{3x-5}{2}$. That error occurs because we did not study fractions well in lower grades."

Eugene said: "It is a common error to add or subtract fractions without changing the denominators to the same. I used to add numerator with numerator, and add denominator with denominator, such as $\dfrac{5}{7}+\dfrac{3}{8}=\dfrac{8}{15}$. Now I know that was not correct."

Maya said: "When I multiplied a fraction by a whole number, I used to multiply the number to both the top and the bottom of the fraction, such as

$\frac{3}{8} \times 7 = \frac{3 \times 7}{8 \times 7}$. This was wrong. The fraction was indeed unchanged. We should view 7 as $\frac{7}{1}$, then top times the top, bottom times the bottom."

Sophie said: "I used to ignore the length of the lines in a composed fraction. Actually $\frac{6}{\frac{3}{4}} = \frac{6 \times 4}{3} = 8$, and $\frac{\frac{6}{3}}{4} = \frac{\frac{6}{3}}{\frac{4}{1}} = \frac{6 \times 1}{3 \times 4} = \frac{6}{12} = \frac{1}{2}$, they are different."

Danny said: "If the price of an object increases 10% then decreases 10%, it looks like the price is unchanged. Actually it is changed. Our school teacher emphasized that difference."

Hall said: "My mistake was to add the same amount to the numerator and the denominator and consider the value as unchanged. Indeed $\frac{7}{8} \neq \frac{7+2}{8+2}$."

Carolyn said: "Not only that, questions like $\frac{2^3 + 1^3}{3^3 + 4^3}$ cannot be simplified as $\frac{2+1}{3+4}$. The former equals $\frac{9}{91}$, while the latter equals $\frac{3}{7}$, they are different."

Dr.C pointed out: "Well, there is an exception. If $b + c = a$, then $\frac{a^3 + b^3}{a^3 + c^3} = \frac{a+b}{a+c}$ is *always* true. For example $3 + 2 = 5$ so $\frac{5^3 + 2^3}{5^3 + 3^3} = \frac{133}{152} = \frac{7}{8}$, while $\frac{5+2}{5+3} = \frac{7}{8}$, both are the same. It can be proved strictly. I would leave this proof for you to do at home as an exercise."

Dr.C also said: "Your examples are useful. We always learn from our own mistakes. Sometimes you may feel that the word problems involving fractions are hard. Let us start with $12 \times \frac{2}{3} = 8$. We can ask three type questions based on this equality.

"The first question is aimed at the number 8. 'What is $\frac{2}{3}$ of 12?'. For example 'Mike has 12 foreign language books. Among them two-thirds are Spanish books. How many Spanish books does Mike have?' The solution is $12 \times \frac{2}{3} = 8$.

"The second question asks about the fraction, 'Nancy has visited 12 foreign countries. Among them 8 countries were in Africa. Please find the fraction of the African countries among all countries she has visited'. To solve it, just write the fraction $\frac{8}{12}$ then simplify it.

"The third question asks about the number 12. For example, 'two thirds of what number is 8?' or 'Robert finished two thirds of today's homework. He finished 8 questions. How many homework questions did he have today?' The solution is $8 \div \frac{2}{3} = 8 \times \frac{3}{2} = 12$.

"We solved the above word problems by three different ways. However, we could solve all of them in one generalized manner. Write them in ratio. The three questions above may be written as $\frac{x}{12} = \frac{2}{3}$, $\frac{x}{100} = \frac{8}{12}$ (to find the percent of the countries), and $\frac{8}{x} = \frac{2}{3}$. So you see, different type fraction problems can be solved either by individual formulas, or by one formula for all of them. Isn't math an interesting subject?"

3.3   A discussion about decimals

A gentle breeze flew over the lawn. Today's class was not held in the usual classroom, instead, students sat around a tree, discussed decimals with Dr.C.

Eugene said first: "Dr.C, I love decimals. Compared to fractions, decimals are so cute and are more welcomed by us, the students. In many cases if you compare two fractions it is not easy to see which one is greater, however, it is very clear to say which decimal is greater. For instance it is hard to compare two fractions like $\frac{14}{19}$ and $\frac{20}{27}$. If we write them in decimals, they become 0.737 and 0.741, so easy to know the latter is greater."

Jenny smiled: "Eugene, you are lazy, aren't you? We all know that using a calculator to evaluate decimals is easier than to evaluate fractions."

Laughter burst out in the crowd. Dr.C followed the trend and led the discussion to more depth: "Certainly, decimal calculations are easier than fraction calculations. When you add or subtract fractions you must convert them into the same denominator first. To add or subtract decimals what you need to do is just to line up the decimal points. However, fractions may give us more accurate results. Although $\frac{2}{5}$ is as accurate as 0.4, $\frac{14}{19}$ however is more accurate than 0.737 because $\frac{14}{19}$ is 0.7368421.....

"When you write decimals, I advise you *not* to write 0.737 as '.737' although many people are doing so everyday. If a pharmacist reads .342 as 342, that would be a very serious mistake, even cost a person's life. Similarly if an architect reads .342 as 342, that would be a disaster too. If you write it as 0.342, the room for that mistake is much smaller.

"One more advantage: when you later study scientific notations, 0.00023 is written as 2.3×10^{-4}. We only need to count how many zeroes are there. 4 zeroes lead to 10^{-4}. If you write the decimal as .00023, you might unfortunately consider it as 2.3×10^{-3} (wrong).

"Always look at one more digit down the road when you round numbers. For instance if you want to round the number 2.046 to the nearest hundredth, your eyes should not stop at the digit 4, but one more digit, the 6. Therefore you should round up the number as 2.05 instead of rounding down to 2.04. The zeroes in a decimal are quite special, if you write 0.015 as 0.0150000, the number is basically the same, if you want to multiply a decimal by 1000 or 10000, just move the decimal point to the right 3 or 4 places; if you want to divide a decimal by 10 or 100, just move the decimal point left 1 or 2 places. When we calculate 1452×21 or 14.52×2.1, if we place the longer number on top, it would be more convenient.

"Limited decimals and infinite recurring decimals can be written as fractions (for example, $0.6 = \dfrac{3}{5}$, $0.3333... = \dfrac{1}{3}$). On the other hand infinite non-recurring decimals cannot be written as fractions (example: π can only be written approximately as $\dfrac{22}{7}$ or $\dfrac{355}{113}$ etc, cannot be written *accurately* as a fraction). On the other hand, every fraction can be written accurately as a decimal (including infinite recurring decimal).

"Who invented the decimals? Several ancient countries contributed to the introduction of decimals. In 1616 John Napier of Scotland first used a point to separate the whole number part and the less than 1 part of a number. Canada has two official languages, English and French. In Canada you may find something interesting: decimal points are written as ',' or '.', depending where you are and what language you use. Therefore both 0.042 and 0,042 are common and correct in Canada.

"Well, today's lesson ends here. Whether you love fractions more or you love decimals more, they are two beautiful flowers in the garden of mathematics. To learn both of them you have two wings, one wing is called 'fractions', and the other is called 'decimals'. You can fly freely with both wings working together for you."

3.4 "Personalities" of decimals and fractions

It was an interesting vivid math class. Dr.C asked the students to compare the "disposition" or "personality" of fractions and decimals.

"What?" asked the students with surprise, "Do fractions and decimals have their own personality?"

"Oh yes," said Dr.C. "Both fractions and decimals are our friends. They are connected to each other. A fraction can be changed into a decimal and vice versa. But --- have you noticed what rules each follows? What 'personality' does each have? What is common to both and what is the difference between them? Such a discussion is inspirational and useful. Percent is a fraction with denominator 100 so it is included in the discussion of fractions.

Lisa said first: "Let me see. A fraction may have another fraction inside, a decimal cannot have another decimal in it. Therefore $\dfrac{\frac{2}{7}}{5}$ is allowed in math, but 11.3.7.1does not have a meaning."

"Good, and I would point out one thing," said Pam. "When we write a composite fraction --- a fraction in a fraction --- be aware which line is longer. The fraction $\dfrac{2}{\frac{3}{7}}$ is different from the fraction $\dfrac{\frac{2}{3}}{7}$. The former one equals $\dfrac{14}{3}$, while the latter one equals $\dfrac{2}{21}$. A more general rule is $\dfrac{\frac{a}{b}}{\frac{c}{d}} = \dfrac{ad}{bc}$, the top ($a$) and the bottom ($d$) go to the top numerator position, and the middle two positions (b and c) become the denominator. The above two fractions can be considered as special cases of this expression, for instance $\dfrac{2}{\frac{3}{7}}$ is the same as $\dfrac{\frac{2}{1}}{\frac{3}{7}}$."

Jack said: "We can find a decimal in a fraction, but not a fraction in a decimal. 0.5% or $\dfrac{0.5}{100}$ are legal in math, however $0.32\frac{4}{5}$ is usually something we try to avoid."

Tina said: "A fraction can only equal to one decimal. For example $\dfrac{4}{5} = 0.8$, to write it as 0.80 or 0.800 is not considered as a new number. On the other hand one decimal can be equal to many fractions, for example 0.4 is equal to $\dfrac{4}{10}, \dfrac{2}{5}, \dfrac{18}{45}$, or $\dfrac{136258}{340645}$, etc."

Peter added: "Any fraction can be written as a decimal. Even a fraction like 1/3 can be written as infinite recurring decimal 0.3333....

However an unlimited, non-recurring decimal like $\pi = 3.14159265...$ cannot be written accurately as a fraction. It can only be approximated as $\dfrac{22}{7}$ or $\dfrac{355}{113}$, etc."

Dr.C listened carefully to the audience then said: "Today's discussion is very good. Through this lesson we gain a deeper understanding of decimals and fractions through our discussion. We see that the 'personalities' of decimals and fractions are different, although they do have some characteristics in common. To be honest, both fractions and decimals are restrained on addition and subtraction, and are more flexible on multiplication and division.

"Let me explain it. When we add or subtract decimals the decimal points must be aligned, otherwise our answer is wrong. When we add or subtract fractions we have to convert them into the same denominator, otherwise our answer is also wrong. If we do $\dfrac{2}{5}+\dfrac{1}{3}$ as $\dfrac{2+1}{5+3}$, we are wrong. Addition and subtraction are strict.

"On the other hand when we multiply two decimals we do not need to line up the decimal points. Indeed we can 'forget' the decimal points, treat them as a multiplication between two whole numbers until we get an answer, then count together how many decimal digits are behind the two decimal points. Fraction multiplication is also more flexible than fraction addition and subtraction. Fraction multiplication does not require a common denominator. You can start right away with different denominators. If you do change two fractions into the same denominator then multiply, you are still correct --- however unnecessary. You can multiply 'top with top', 'bottom with bottom', or you can first cancel common factors from the top and the bottom, either way. Dividing a fraction is the same as multiplying the reciprocal of a fraction, both multiplication and division are quite flexible. The comparison between fractions and decimals is quite interesting.

"In many practical cases we care about significant digits. The rules of significant digits are as follows: When quantities are being added or subtracted the number of decimal places (not significant digits) in the answer should be the same as the least number of decimal places in any of the numbers being added or subtracted (comment: watch the decimal places). In multiplication and division the number of significant digits in an answer should equal the least number of significant digits in any one of the numbers being multiplied or divided. (comment: decimal places are not important) ."

3.5   How can we find *all* factors of a number?

Certainly, one may find all factors of a whole number by checking factors one by one. Such as: can this number be divided by 2? divided by 3? This way is slow. It is easy to miss some factors. Brenda and Susan try to find a better way to do it.

Susan uses a "factor tree". For example the number 100 can be written as the product of prime numbers ($100 = 2 \times 2 \times 5 \times 5$), therefore 2, 5, 25, 50 and 100 are factors of 100. The following tree diagram can express the relationship.

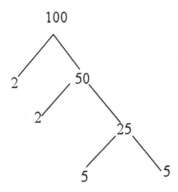

100

2   50

2

25

5   5

"However, in your factor tree diagram there is no number 4 and no number 20. We know that 4 and 20 both are factors of 100," says Brenda. "Our goal is to find *all* factors of a number, not some of them."

"Thanks", says Susan. "Do you have a better method?"

Brenda says: "My method is not to check factors one by one, that way is too slow. Instead of checking 1, 2, 3, my way is to squeeze from both ends towards the middle, until we arrive at a step such that we are unable to squeeze further. Use 60 as an example:

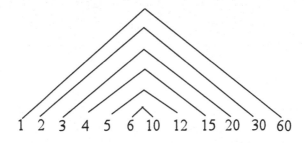

1 2 3 4 5 6 10 12 15 20 30 60

"The numbers 1 and 60 make a pair ($1 \times 60 = 60$). Next pair is 2 and 30, then 3 and 20, 4 and 15, 5 and 12, and 6 and 10. Can we go even further? No, because between 6 and 10 we only have 7, 8, and 9, they are not factors of 60. So the job is done, we get all factors of 60, without missing any."

"Good method!" says Susan. "If the whole number is a perfect square number, then at the end of squeezing a number will multiply itself. The following diagram shows the result of the perfect square number 81 (9×9 at the last step)."

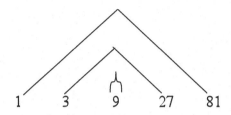

3.6 Obtaining the GCF and the LCM at the same time

Doris and Karl calculated the GCF (the greatest common factor) and the LCM (the least common multiple) of two given numbers. Karl's method was to find all factors of these two numbers first, then circle the common ones, and finally to find the greatest one among the common factors (the GCF). Doris multiplied each given number by 2, by 3, by 4, etc, and compared the products to see which multiple comes first in both lists (the LCM).

They complained that these ways were too slow. Dr.C said: "There is a better method. We can calculate the GCF and the LCM of two numbers at once. Do you want to know that?"

Both Doris and Karl wanted to know, so Dr.C used 36 and 48 as an example to find the GCF and the LCM of these two numbers.

$$\begin{array}{r|cc} 2 & 36 & 48 \\ \hline 2 & 18 & 24 \\ \hline 3 & 9 & 12 \\ \hline & 3 & 4 \end{array}$$

"Write down the two numbers 36 and 48. Both of them are even numbers so they can both be divided by 2. Write 2 on the left side. The answers are 18 and 24, write them below 36 and 48. Continue, divide 18 and 24 by 2 then by 3, and go on this process until you cannot go further. At the bottom you have 3 and 4. The numbers 3 and 4 can only be divided by 1, and the results are still 3 and 4 so we stop.

"Now the product of the numbers *on the left side* (2, 2, 3) is the GCF. The product of the numbers *on the left side and at the bottom* (2, 2, 3, 3, 4) is the LCM"

GCF $= 2 \times 2 \times 3 = 12$

LCM $= 2 \times 2 \times 3 \times 3 \times 4 = 144$

"If we start by dividing the two numbers by 6 or 12, we could finish faster," said Dr.C. "This method of course was not invented by me, indeed many school teachers are using it every day. I only want to point out one thing: If there are three or more numbers, using this way we can still find the correct GCF, however the LCM found by this way may not be correct. For example:

$$\begin{array}{r|ccc} 6 & 12 & 18 & 24 \\ \hline & 2 & 3 & 4 \end{array}$$

GCF $= 6$ (correct)

LCM $= 6 \times 2 \times 3 \times 4 = 144$ (incorrect. LCM should be 72)

63

"Therefore if there are more than 2 numbers, we do not apply this method to find the LCM, unless we ask ourselves whether the LCM found in this way can be further reduced."

3.7 Games with prime numbers and ratios

Today Dr.C led his students to play two games. First he told each student to write whole numbers 1 to 100 on a piece of paper, then asked them to circle all prime numbers.

The classroom was quiet, only the sound of paper rustling could be heard. Nonie, Stephan and Clare finished first. Dr.C did not check their results, instead, he told them to count: "How many prime numbers have you got?"

Between 1 and 100, Clare got 25, Stephan got 27, and Nonie got 24 prime numbers.

"The correct number of primes within 100 is 25," said Dr.C. "Clare got 25, that fact does not guarantee that she is all right, because she may get one or two extras and omit one or two correct prime numbers. As to Stephan and Nonie, sorry, something must be wrong. One of you got too many and the other too few."

After a while, Nonie found the missing number 53, Stephan understood that 87 and 91 were not prime numbers. For 87, $8+7 = 15$; since 15 can be divided by 3 so 87 can be divided by 3 too. For 91, since $13 \times 7 = 91$, and 91 can be divided by 7 and 13. Clare checked her 25 numbers and found that she was all right. She got the 25 numbers by first deleting all even numbers except 2, all numbers ending with 0 or 5 except 5 itself, and all numbers whose sum of digits could be divided by 3, then considered which of the rest could be divided by 7. After those work she ended with the correct 25 prime numbers.

Dr.C told the students a story: "The number $n^2 - n + 41$ is a prime number for $n = 1$, $n = 2$, $n = 3$, etc., until $n = 40$ (when $n = 40$, $n^2 - n + 41 = 1601$). Then when $n = 41$, a problem occurs: $41^2 - 41 + 41 = 41^2 = 1681$. Since 1681 can be divided by 41, it is no longer a prime number. So, even if it is correct for many values of n, we still cannot guarantee that it is a truth. From 1 to 100 exactly 1/4 are primes, that does not guarantee that from 101 to 200 exactly 1/4 will be prime numbers. Please find out how many prime numbers are there between 101 and 200, do it as homework.

"There is another game," said Dr.C. "This time use two fingers. We know how to solve a ratio question. For example $2 : 5 = x : 30$ can be written in fraction form $\dfrac{2}{5} = \dfrac{x}{30}$, then we can find the answer by cross-multiplication $5x = 2 \times 30$, so $x = 12$. If there are three terms on each side such as $4 : a : 18 = b : 33 : 27$, it is hard to be written in fraction form. What can we do? Don't worry, please use the index fingers of your two hands to *cover the same term* (the first, the second, or the last term) on each side. If we cover the first term from *both* sides, the above expression becomes $a : 18 = 33 : 27$. A tap of finger makes the question easier. We know how to solve $a : 18 = 33 : 27$ by fraction method (cross-multiplication) and the answer is $a = 22$. Similarly if we cover the middle terms from both sides, the problem becomes $4 : 18 = b : 27$ and $b = 6$. Longer ratio problems can be solved in this way --- converting hard to easy, converting unfamiliar things into familiar things."

"Simple! Just a tap of fingers and we know how to solve the problem!" said the students.

Chapter 4
More Geometry

4.1 Minimum or maximum overlapping

Dr.C drew a diagram on the board and said:"In this diagram a figure is made by using toothpicks. Please move three toothpicks so that you have 5 squares of the same size left."

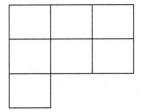

Dr.C said: "To do this let us think about it first. A square has four sides. In the diagram there are 20 toothpicks, just perfect to make 4 squares. If a square shares a common side with another square we do not need 20. Therefore in this question there should not be any overlapping, otherwise we would need less than 20, not 20 toothpicks. The result after the displacement is shown below, (3 dashed line segments are displaced to the wavy line positions)."

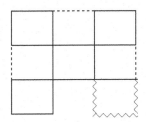

67

"Well, in some other cases we may need as much overlapping as possible," said Dr.C. "Let us consider another question. Ten students stand in five straight lines, in each line there are four students. How can they do it? Obviously this question is impossible without overlapping. $5 \times 4 = 20$, without overlapping we would need 20 students, not 10. Only when one stands on two lines can we increase the effect and satisfy the requirement with less number of students. Thus the result is a five angle star as shown below.

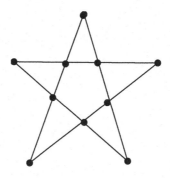

"Compare the two problems, we see sometimes we need no overlapping at all, and sometimes we need the maximum overlapping. In other cases like the Venn diagram questions, we also need overlapping to solve problems."

Dr.C said: "When you solve problems don't panic, don't be nervous. Think about it first, slow down at the starting point. This way looks slow but actually may help you work faster. Otherwise you may go down the wrong path and lose sight of the correct solution.

Finally Dr.C said: "Consider a question. If Barbara has six different type of pets, each type 10 ($10a, 10b, 10c, 10d, 10e, 10f$), and she wants to build a 15 room pet house, how can she put four *different* pets into each room so that no room has exactly the same combination as another room? This is not hard, start from *abc*, then she may have *abcd*, *abce* and *abcf*. Then start from *abd* and get *abde* and *abdf* , and so on. This is a combination problem, choose 4 from 6 different elements (order not important) then there are 15 different choices. Each two cells have some overlapping but not completely the same combination.

4.2 The altitude on the hypotenuse of a right triangle

Dr.C drew a right triangle △*ABC* on the board with angle *A* as the right angle. He then drew the altitude *AD* on the hypotenuse *BC* . He told the class: "Given that *AB* = 24*cm* and *AC* = 10*cm* , please find the length of the altitude *AD*."

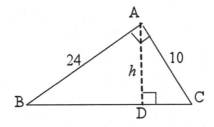

Not long later the students found the length *AD* in several ways. The answer was *AD* = 9.23*cm* .

Robert used area in his calculation. The area of △*ABC* is $\frac{1}{2}(AB)(AC) = \frac{1}{2} \times 24 \times 10 = 120cm^2$. The same triangle area can be found by $\frac{1}{2}(AD)(BC)$ too. Robert applied the Pythagorean theorem to find the length of the hypotenuse $BC = \sqrt{AB^2 + AC^2} = 26cm$, therefore $\frac{1}{2} \times AD \times 26 = 120$ and $AD = 9.23cm$.

Lisa used similar triangles. $\Delta ABC \sim \Delta DBA$, so $\dfrac{AC}{DA} = \dfrac{BC}{BA}$, that is $\dfrac{10}{DA} = \dfrac{26}{24}$, and $AD = DA = 9.23cm$.

Dr.C gave his comment: "Lisa's method considered similar triangles. To apply similar triangle method the key is the *first* step, ΔABC is similar to ΔDBA and ΔDAC . Here *the order is important*. Look at the diagram you see that getting the correct order is not obvious. A wrong order leads to a wrong answer. Point A is the vertex of the right angle, therefore on the right side the first letter D must also represent the vertex of another right angle. The second letter is the vertex of the smallest angle (B in ΔABC and ΔDBA ; A in ΔDAC). Once we have the correct order $\Delta ABC \sim \Delta DBA$, the rest is easy. From there we have $\dfrac{AC}{DA} = \dfrac{BC}{BA}$. On the left side we have the 1st vertex (A in ΔABC, D in ΔDBA) and the 3rd vertex (C in ΔABC, A in ΔDBA); on the right side we have the 2nd vertex and the 3rd vertex."

Nancy's method was to apply the law of cosine. In ΔABC $10^2 = 26^2 + 24^2 - 2(26)(24)\cos B$, and the solution was $\angle B = 22.6°$. Then she turned to ΔABD and found that $AD = 24\sin B = 9.23cm$. Tim pointed out that the angle $\angle B$ can be found in an easier way, since ΔABC is a right triangle, we could use the definition of tangent instead of the cosine law and got $\tan B = \dfrac{10}{24}$ so that $\angle B = 22.6°$. This method requires the knowledge of trigonometry.

Frank tried a different approach. He drew a circle whose center O is the mid-point of the line segment BC and he set BC as a diameter. Since $\angle A$ is a right angle, point A must be on the circle.

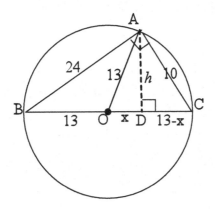

Frank said: "Assume $OD = x$, then $DC = 13 - x$ (13 is the radius of the circle since the diameter $BC = 26cm$). In $\triangle AOD$, $AD^2 = 13^2 - x^2$, in $\triangle ACD$ we have $AD^2 = 10^2 - (13 - x)^2$, therefore $13^2 - x^2 = 10^2 - (13 - x)^2$. The solution is $x = 9.15cm$ hence $AD = 9.23cm$."

There is a proverb saying "*All roads lead to Rome*". In today's class, students used different approaches to solve the same problem and all arrived at the correct solution.

4.3 π is not an integer, why not?

Tom asked Dr.C: "Why is π, the ratio of the circumference to the diameter of a circle, not an integer? If π were an integer, that would be wonderful!"

"Oh yes," said Dr.C. "It would be great if π is an integer. All formulas about the area and the circumference of a circle would be simplified. We would not need a calculator to evaluate the circumference or area of a circle. What wonderful news that would be! However, I must regret to say that this is not possible. Indeed π *cannot be* a simple integer. Let me prove it.

"First, let us prove that π cannot be a number equal to or greater than 4. In the following diagram there is a circle and its circumscribed square. The area of the circle is πr^2. The side length of the square is $2r$ and the area of the square is $4r^2$. Which area is greater? Obviously the square is greater so π must be less than 4.

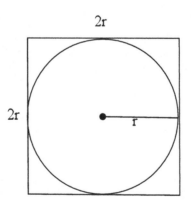

"Next, let us prove that π must be greater than 3. In the following diagram there is a circle and its inscribed hexagon. The circumference of the circle is $2\pi r$. Whether π is or is not an integer this is always true because π

is defined as the ratio of the circumference to the diameter of any circle. One sixth of the circumference of the circle is $\frac{1}{3}\pi r$, that is the length of the arc *ACB*. For a regular hexagon each internal angle is **60°**, therefore triangle OAB is an equilateral triangle of side length $AB = r$.

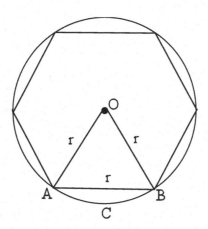

"Which one is longer, the arc *ACB*, or the straight line AB? Of course the curve is longer. So $\frac{1}{3}\pi r > r$, this means $\pi > 3$.

"Now that $\pi > 3$ and $\pi < 4$, we have to say, with regret that π must be between 3 and 4 and cannot be an integer.

"Such a conclusion can also be obtained from direct measurement. Measure the diameter and the circumference of any circle and compare the results. In the above we proved the conclusion by logic, by mathematics."

4.4   Figures made from straight lines and curves

Dr.C discussed geometry with his students: "It is well known that a rectangle of fixed length perimeter has the maximum area when its shape is a square. Similarly if the area is fixed, the perimeter would be the minimum when the shape of a rectangle is a square. Based on these, can we claim that a square has the maximum area among all shapes of the same perimeter?"

After serious consideration the students got the correct conclusion: "No". Victor said: "The shape that produces the maximum possible area from the same perimeter is not a square, instead it is a circle. If the length of a thread is a, the radius of the circle is $r = \dfrac{a}{2\pi}$, and the area of the circle is $\pi r^2 = \dfrac{a^2}{4\pi} \approx 0.0796a^2$. If we use the same thread to form a square, its side length is $\dfrac{a}{4}$ and its area would be $\dfrac{a^2}{16} = 0.0625a^2$. The ratio of the circle area to the square area is 1.27:1."

Dr.C pointed out: "This example can be stated in another way. If a square has the same area as a circle, the perimeter of the square must be greater than the circumference of the circle. Note that now the circumference ratio is not 1.27:1 (obtained above). We raise the question in the opposite way, but the ratio is not changed from 1.27: 1 to 1: 1.27. The ratio of the perimeter of the square to the circumference of the circle is 1.13:1, not 1.27:1.

"Similar situation can be found in 3-D. It can be proved that when the total surface area of a cylinder (including the two ends) is given, its volume is the smallest when the cross-section of the cylinder is a square ($h = 2r$). However, if we consider this volume is the maximum possible volume of a 3-D object with the given surface area, then the answer is a sphere, not a cylinder. Just like a circle in 2-D, in 3-D a sphere has the maximum symmetry.

"To get the maximum volume when its total surface area is fixed, or vice versa to get the minimum surface area when its volume is fixed, we need maximum symmetry. The situation is clear in the following table.

	$SA=100cm^2$	$V=100cm^3$
cube	$V=68.0cm^3$	$SA=129.3cm^2$
cylinder with $h=2r$	$V=76.8cm^3$	$SA=119.7cm^2$
sphere	$V=93.9cm^3$	$SA=104.2cm^2$

"In physics when there is no external force, due to the liquid surface tension a drop of liquid automatically takes the shape of a sphere, which has the minimum surface area for the same volume.

"If we cut a 100 cm long wire into two pieces, bend one piece to make a circle and bend the other piece to make a square, we would get the following results.

Requirement	Square part (cm)	Circle part (cm)
The circle and the square should have the same area	53	47
The circle and the square should have the same perimeter	50	50
The total area of the circle and the square is the minimum	56	44
The total area of the circle and the square is the maximum	0	100

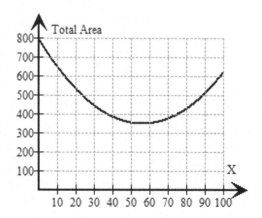

"The horizontal coordinate x shows how to cut the 100 cm long wire, from 0 to x is used to make the square, and the other part (from x to 100 cm) is used to make the circle. For example, $x = 60$ means that we use 60 cm to make the square, and use the rest (40 cm) to make the circle. The vertical coordinate y is the total area of the circle and the square in units of cm^2.

"A circle in 2-D and a sphere in 3-D are quite special in geometry," said Dr.C. "A circle has infinite lines of symmetry and is the most regular shape in 2-D. A sphere has infinite lines of symmetry and is the most regular shape in 3-D. Our ancestors realized the importance of circles and spheres. Using a ruler without calibration plus a compass, we can construct many geometric figures, we can locate the mid-point of a line segment; divide an angle into two equal halves (but not 3 equal one-thirds); we can locate various centers of a triangle. Although a straight line and a curve both contain infinite number of points, a curve can be proved to contain more points than a straight line (reference: the book 'One, Two, Three,....Infinity' by George Gamow). When our knowledge of the world developed from straight line figures to curved figures, our understanding of the world advanced up one big step."

4.5   Regular and irregular figures

After teaching the previous section, Dr.C felt that he had more to say. The next day he reminded the class: "Circles and spheres are the most regular shapes in 2-D and 3-D geometry respectively. A triangle could be regular (an equilateral triangle), or irregular (an arbitrary triangle). A quadrilateral could be regular (a square), or irregular too. One common mistake of beginners is to draw the diagram of a problem *too regular* without a reason. If the problem only states 'a triangle', don't draw an isosceles or an equilateral triangle, otherwise you may mislead yourself (example: you may get the wrong impression that the median on the bottom side is perpendicular to that side). If the question only tells you a triangle and you draw a figure which looks like a right triangle, you might wrongly think that the three sides satisfy the Pythagorean Theorem. If you draw a quadrilateral as a trapezoid or a parallelogram, you mislead yourself too. When you draw two lines parallel to each other without a reason, you may think that they do not intersect each other. As a rule of thumb, when you do geometry problems please do not draw figures too special without a correct reason."

"If the question has constraints, then use them, pay attention to them. Sometimes these constraints may be hidden. For example, can you find the perimeter of an isosceles triangle whose two sides are 11.8 cm and 23.6 cm?"

Wendy said: "I got two answers, 47.2 cm and 59.0 cm (11.8+11.8+23.6=47.2, or 11.8+23.6+23.6=59.0)."

Millie said: "No, that is incorrect. Both answers seem to have considered that the triangle is isosceles, but 11.8+11.8+23.6 cm cannot make a triangle. There is a hidden requirement, in any triangle the sum of any two side lengths should be longer than the third side. Now 23.6 is exactly twice as 11.8, so that 11.8+11.8+23.6 triangle is impossible. Only the other answer 11.8+23.6+23.6=59.0 cm is possible."

"What Millie pointed out is important. That error was not obvious," said Dr.C. "Regular and irregular things are related to each other. A famous example is that in *any* triangle if you draw a line segment to connect the mid-points of two sides, the line segment is parallel to the third side and equal to half of the length of the third side. Just think about it, starting from an arbitrary shape irregular triangle, the answer is so regular.

"More than that, starting from an arbitrary shape irregular quadrilateral if you connect the four mid-points, you will always get a regular figure ---a parallelogram."

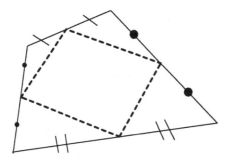

Dr.C said: "We know, two parallel lines never intersect each other. That is correct in plane geometry. But do you know, this conclusion is not always true in the real world?"

"Really?" doubted the students.

Dr.C smiled and explained: "Here is a model of our Earth. On this globe we can learn many interesting things that do not exist in plane geometry. In a plane the shortest distance between two points is the straight-line segment connecting the two points. Parallel lines do not meet. These conclusions however are not true on a sphere. All longitudes of our globe Earth meet at two points --- the North Pole and the South Pole. Therefore in non-plane geometry parallel lines do meet. The sum of three internal angles in a triangle may be greater than 180° or less than 180° depending on what type of curved surface it is. In non-Euclidean geometry a limited but infinite boundary is possible. I suggest that interested students may study non-Euclidean geometry from the Internet."

4.6   Kirchhoff's rule

Dr.C drew a map on the board. He said: "Look at this traffic intersection. If 5 cars entered the intersection from west, 3 cars came from east, and 1 car left the intersection going north, how many cars went south from that intersection?"

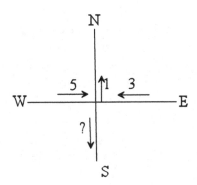

Because 8 cars (5+3 = 8) entered the intersection, 8 cars had to go out from that intersection. As a result $8-1=7$ cars should leave the intersection going south. This is the "junction rule", an analogy of the famous "Kirchhoff's junction rule" in electric circuit theory. There the physics rule states that "the net current flowing into a junction equals the net current flowing out of the same junction". (In physics there is another Kirchhoff's rule, the loop rule, which we do not need here).

Then Dr.C showed the class two more complicated maps. On each map the numbers and the arrows showed how many cars were moving in that direction. He asked the students to apply the Kirchhoff's junction rule and input numbers on all roads.

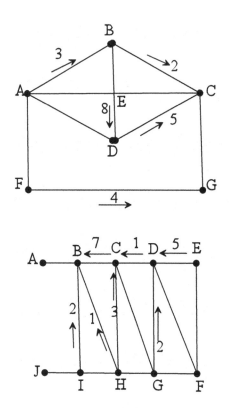

Answers:

[1] D to A 3, E to A 4, B to E 1, C to E 11.

[2] B to A 10, J to I 10, I to H 8, H to G 4, F to G 1, F to E 5, D to F 6, G to C 3.

Chapter 5
Mean Values, Statistics

5.1 The mean values

Linda and friends study the mean values in school. To find the mean value of two numbers just add them and divide the sum by 2, to find the mean value of three numbers just add them and divide the sum by 3, etc.

Today Dr.C said: "Sometimes this method does not work."

"Assume that a person goes up a hill then comes down the same hill back to the original position, her speed up hill is v_1 and down hill is v_2, her average speed up and down the hill is *not* $\dfrac{v_1 + v_2}{2}$."

Dr.C used his special way called **'pushing the case to its extreme'** to explain: "This case becomes very clear if we use an extremely large number for the down hill speed v_2. Assume that the speed to go up hill is 1 m/s, and assume that the speed to go down hill is 1000 m/s (extremely large, imagine that you sit in a rocket and fly down hill). If the hill is 100 m long you need 100 seconds to go up. The time to go down is only 0.1 sec. Altogether you need 100.1 sec to go up and down. The total length is 200 m.

Now do you notice that there is a problem? The result of $\dfrac{v_1 + v_2}{2}$ is

$\dfrac{1 + 1000}{2} = 500.5$ m/s. If you *really* use this average speed to go for 200 m distance, the time needed would be only 0.3996 sec, less than 0.4 sec. However remember that only to go up hill you already spent 100 sec time. Therefore the calculated average speed must be wrong, cannot be as large as 500.5 m/s.

"The correct way to calculate average speed is to divide the total distance (200 m) by the total time (100.1 sec), the result is 1.998 m/s. Use our 'pushing the case to its extreme' method it becomes obvious at a glance."

Among many ways of teaching, this way was the most convincing method. Linda learned this method quickly, she said: "We can also assume that the speed to go down the hill is 1 m/s, while the speed to go up is so slow that it takes 10 years to go up that hill (exaggerated!). Then $\frac{v_1 + v_2}{2}$ would produce an answer (almost) $\frac{0+1}{2}$, that is 0.5 m/s. If this is the average speed, to go up and down hill needs $200 \div 0.5 = 400$ seconds. However we know that to go up alone needs 10 years time. So the answer 400 sec cannot be true. We cannot calculate the average speed by $\frac{v_1 + v_2}{2}$."

"Excellent," said Dr.C. "A ship goes upstream then downstream on a river. Such a question is similar to the one we discuss here. The average speed also cannot be found by the arithmetic mean $\frac{v_1 + v_2}{2}$."

"In addition to the arithmetic mean, in our daily life we sometimes need to find the mean *with weights*. Multiply every item by its assigned weight, add, and then divide the result by the number of items. Another mean is the geometric mean $\sqrt{a_1 a_2}$, or $\sqrt[3]{a_1 a_2 a_3}$ etc. Many of us may feel that a geometric mean should be greater than an arithmetic mean since numbers increase faster geometrically compared to arithmetically. Actually

82

in case that there is no negative numbers the arithmetic mean of given numbers is *always* no less than the geometric mean. For instance $\dfrac{3+13}{2} = 8$, while $\sqrt{3 \times 13} \approx 6.245$. If negative numbers are allowed, this is no longer true. The arithmetic mean of (-3) and (-13) is (-8), and their geometric mean is 6.245, greater than any negative number."

Linda and friends also tried many other interesting mean value questions. For example, could the mean of two numbers be equal to one of the two given numbers? Could the average be less than (or greater than) both given numbers? Could the average equal to one half of a given number? Could the mean of two numbers be zero? When one of two numbers was given and the average of the two numbers was also given, could we find the unknown number? Students discussed those questions with great interest.

5.2   Mean, median, mode and range of fractions

The mean, median, and mode are called the 3M. For example if we have five numbers 2, 7, 6, 2, and 3, their 3M and R are:

mean $= (2 + 7 + 6 + 2 + 3) \div 5 = 4$ (the arithmetic average)

median $= 3$ (the middle one of 2, 2, 3, 6, 7; or the average of the middle two numbers if there are even number of numbers)

mode $= 2$ (the number appears most times. A question may have no mode (e.g., 1, 2, 7) or more than one mode (e.g., 1, 2, 2, 6, 6).

Range $= 7 - 2 = 5$ (the difference between the greatest and the smallest numbers)

If the numbers given are fractions the question becomes harder. For example find the 3M and R of the following seven fractions.

$$\frac{7}{10} \quad \frac{5}{12} \quad \frac{4}{20} \quad \frac{1}{4} \quad \frac{1}{6} \quad \frac{2}{5} \quad \frac{1}{5}$$

Now the 3M and R are not obvious. To find the answers we change them to the same denominator first --- in this question the least common denominator is 60.

$$\frac{42}{60} \quad \frac{25}{60} \quad \frac{12}{60} \quad \frac{15}{60} \quad \frac{10}{60} \quad \frac{24}{60} \quad \frac{12}{60}$$

Now the question becomes clear. Since every fraction has the same denominator we need only to look at the numerators. The question now is simplified to a whole number question, find the 3M and R of the seven whole numbers 42, 25, 12, 15, 10, 24, and 12. The answer of the mean value is 20, therefore the mean of the original question is $\frac{20}{60}$ or $\frac{1}{3}$. Similarly we can find and simplify other answers, they are: median $= \frac{1}{4}$, mode $= \frac{1}{5}$, and range $= \frac{8}{15}$.

Having discussed the above, Dr.C adds: "It is more difficult to go backwards. If you have seven fractions (in order from small to large) A, B, C ,D, E, F, G, among them we know that the greatest one (G) is $\frac{3}{5}$, the mean is $\frac{1}{3}$; there are two modes $\frac{1}{6}$ and $\frac{8}{15}$, plus we know that the range is $\frac{8}{15}$. Please write down the seven fractions.

"The way to solve this problem is again to convert all denominators to the same. Using 30 as the common denominator, the question becomes: the greatest one (G) is $\dfrac{18}{30}$, the mean is $\dfrac{10}{30}$, the 2 modes are $\dfrac{5}{30}$ and $\dfrac{16}{30}$, and the range is $\dfrac{16}{30}$. Since every fraction has the same denominator 30, we can concentrate on the numerators only.

"Only check the numerators, the greatest one is 18 and the range is 16, therefore the minimum numerator must be 2. We write the 7 numerators as 2, B, C, D, E, F, 18.

"Since the modes are 5 and 16, the seven numerators could be 2, 5, 5, D, 16, 16, 18. In order to get the mean number 10, the value of D must be 8. Therefore the seven numerators are 2, 5, 5, 8, 16, 16, 18 Since the common denominator is 30, after we simplify the fractions the answers to the original question are $\dfrac{1}{15}$, $\dfrac{1}{6}$, $\dfrac{1}{6}$, $\dfrac{4}{15}$, $\dfrac{8}{15}$, $\dfrac{8}{15}$, and $\dfrac{3}{5}$."

5.3   Calculating standard deviation using a table

Standard deviation is a useful concept in statistics. Two distributions may have the same mean value μ but different standard deviation σ. The quantity σ tells us whether the distribution is concentrated around the mean value μ or is scattered. The formula to evaluate standard deviation is complicated. We can use a table instead of the formula to evaluate the standard deviation σ, to do so there are two methods.

In this example, find the standard deviation of the six given numbers 1, 2, 4, 4, 9, and 10. Here x means the data given, μ is the mean value, σ^2 is the variance and σ is the standard deviation.

x	$x - \mu$	$(x - \mu)^2$
1	-4	16
2	-3	9
4	-1	1
4	-1	1
9	4	16
10	5	25
sum=30, $n = 6$, $\mu = \frac{30}{6} = 5$		sum=68, $\div$ n get the variance

Thus, the variance is $\sigma^2 = 68 \div 6 = 11.33$ and the standard deviation $\sigma = \sqrt{11.33} = 3.37$. We can also use another method:

x	x^2
1	1
2	4
4	16
4	16
9	81
10	100
sum=30, $\mu = \frac{30}{6} = 5$	sum $= 218$

The variance is $\sigma^2 = \frac{218}{6} - 5^2 = 11.33$ and the standard deviation is $\sigma = \sqrt{11.33} = 3.37$, same as above. This method works even faster than the first method.

Through this lesson the students have learned an easy way to evaluate the standard deviation. They also understand the meaning and the importance of variance and standard deviation in statistics.

5.4 A wide range discussion about statistics

Today is a fine day. Dr.C played volleyball with his students then returned to the classroom, and had a wide range discussion about various aspects of statistics.

[1] Jonathan's question

My group has 7 students. In a recent exam we did very well, the team average was 92. Many members of our team got even higher mark than the team average. Among them, Erika's mark was 4 points higher than the team average, Peter's mark was 1 point higher, Stuart's mark was 3 points higher, Lindsay's mark was 4 points higher than the team average, Ingrid and Timothy's marks were the same as the team average, and mine was 1 point higher than the team average.

What is your impression about our successful team?

[2] Ryan's question

Recently I did some investigation work and used my knowledge of statistics to analyze the data. I went to the traffic control department of our city police office and calculated statistics on the traffic accidents in our city last year. I found a conclusion that more accidents happened inside the city than in the countryside. Later I went to another police department and found that in the last ten years we had more minor incidents (theft, for example) than murder cases. After that I returned to our school and talked with the Principal and the Vice Principal to draw the conclusion that for the same student the correlation between her or his math mark and science mark is higher than the correlation between the literature mark and math mark. Also our physical education teacher told me that the stronger a person is, the heavier she or he can lift weights.

What is your comment on this?

[3] Brendan's question

If you randomly pick a student from the male students of our school, the probability that this person wears glasses is 1/5. If you randomly pick a student from all students of our school, the probability that this person is a male student who wears glasses is 1/4.

What comments would you like to say?

[4] Aaron's question

Four friends A, B, C and D compared their cars. They started at the same time and same place, A and D drove to a nearby location while C and B drove to a farther place. C and D arrived at their destinations at the same time. Sometimes later A and B arrived at their destinations at the same time. C used the same amount of gas as D; while B used the same amount of gas as A. The amount of gas used by B was more than the amount used by D.

Facing so much information and no specific numbers at all, how can we find out which car is the best? Which car is the worst? If a car runs faster and consumes less fuel, it is considered as a good car. If a car uses more fuel and runs less distance it is a bad car.

[Answers]

[1] It is impossible. In a group it is impossible that every body's mark was either higher than or equal to the team average. If someone is higher, there must be at least one person whose mark is lower than the team average.

[2] No doubt that all conclusions are correct, but those conclusions are obvious and therefore not very useful. We better spend time on questions whose answers are not clear yet. A study of these type questions might lead to new discoveries and are usually more significant.

[3] The data given is inconsistent. With conditions the probability must be greater than the probability without conditions. 1/5 is less than 1/4 so that something must be wrong.

Adding conditions always reduces the number of total qualified candidates, therefore increases the probability. Here is another example: 1/100 of the students in our school has first name Wendy, then the probability that a female student in our school happens to have the first name Wendy must be higher than 1/100, because we can exclude all male students in the latter case.

[4] C is the best and A is the worst.

Although no specific number is given, we can still draw two diagrams to compare their properties.

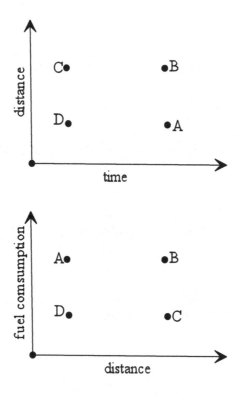

From the first figure we know C is the fastest (short time, long distance). From the second figure we know C used less amount of gasoline for a longer distance.

Therefore car C is the best. Similarly car A is the worst among the four cars.

Chapter 6
Integers, Exponents, Factoring

6.1   A better order to teach integer operations

In all textbooks, in all schools, the operation of positive and negative integers is taught in the traditional order: $+ - \times \div$. Teach integer addition first, then integer subtraction, then multiplication and division. This order seems to be perfectly justified. No one ever challenged it.

However, is this really the best order?

Dr.C says: "I doubt. I have a better idea."

Here is what he says:

[Addition is basic]

There are four and only four cases to do an integer addition: positive plus positive, positive plus negative, negative plus positive, and negative plus negative. There are many ways to teach integer addition. Consider $(+2) + (-5)$ as an example, it may mean a move to the right 2 steps then a move to the left 5 steps on a number line; or to go 2 steps upstairs then 5 steps downstairs. We may also consider a "chess game", with red and black pieces. Assume that black pieces represent positive numbers and red pieces represent negative numbers, then $(-2) + (-3) = -5$ because 2 red pieces meet three red pieces, the result is 5 red pieces (and similarly 2 + 3 = 5, all black pieces). As to $(+2)+(-3)=-1$, 2 black pieces "fight" with 3 red pieces, after one-to-one cancellation there will only be 1 red piece left (similarly we can explain why $(-2)+(+3)=+1$).

[Multiplication and division are easy]

Same sign yields a positive answer, two opposite signs yield a negative answer. That's all, very simple.

[Subtraction is hard]

Subtraction is hard. The usual way is to teach the students that "subtracting an integer is the same as adding its opposite", therefore $(+2)-(+8)=(+2)+(-8)=-6$. We see many students cross out the minus sign, change it to a plus sign, and cross out the plus sign of (+8), change it to (-8). That process is messy and not simple, making the work hard to read!

[Dr.C's method]

Therefore, Dr.C suggests using a new order to teach integer operations: $+\times\div-$, that is, teach addition first, then multiplication and division together, finally teach integer subtraction.

Why this way?

Addition is the most basic operation. Students must learn addition first to really understand negative numbers. Multiplication and division are easy and have the same rules for signs.

How to teach integer subtraction? Our new method is, to view subtraction and addition as **"multiplication of signs"**. Step 1 is to open all brackets. When we open the brackets, we **multiply the signs**. For example, $(+2) - (-5) - (+3)$ is changed to $2 + 5 - 3$. Here we consider $-(-5)$ as +5 because "when negative times negative the result is positive." Also we consider $-(+3)$ as -3, since "when negative times positive, the result is negative."

Let's study another example $(-1) + (-2) - (-6) = -1 - 2 + 6 = -3 + 6 = 3$. Here **the first step is to open all brackets**, same as above. The second step is to collect same sign terms. **Collect all positive numbers together. Collect all negative numbers together.** Thus for whatever long expressions only one positive number and one negative number left after step 2. The third step is to get the final answer: 3 red pieces of the chess meet 6 black pieces, due to cancellation the result should be 3 black pieces (+3).

If you do not try, you do not know how good it is. This $+ \times \div -$ method is very effective. **This method has a brilliant feature: the longer and more complicated the expression is, the more powerful and simpler this method shows.** Learn addition first, then multiplication and division, finally subtraction. Using this method even a student who just began to study integers can perform calculations with *many* integers very fast.

Here is an example. First we do it in the *normal way*:

$$(+3)-(-2)-(+7)+(-1)+(-6)-(+2)+(-3)-(-8)-(+1)$$
$$=(+3)+(+2)-(+7)+(-1)+(-6)-(+2)+(-3)-(-8)-(+1)$$
$$=(+5)-(+7)+(-1)+(-6)-(+2)+(-3)-(-8)-(+1)$$
$$=(+5)+(-7)+(-1)+(-6)-(+2)+(-3)-(-8)-(+1)$$
$$=(-2)+(-1)+(-6)-(+2)+(-3)-(-8)-(+1)$$
$$=(-3)+(-6)-(+2)+(-3)-(-8)-(+1)$$
$$=(-9)-(+2)+(-3)-(-8)-(+1)$$
$$=(-9)+(-2)+(-3)-(-8)-(+1)$$
$$=(-11)+(-3)-(-8)-(+1)$$
$$=(-14)-(-8)-(+1)$$
$$=(-14)+(+8)-(+1)$$
$$=(-6)-(+1)$$
$$=(-6)+(-1)$$
$$=(-7)$$

(What a long and difficult process it is!)

This process is too long. The normal way to do it is to evaluate math bit by bit. First we calculate $(+3)-(-2)$. Because subtract a number is equivalent to add the opposite number, we change it to $(+3)+(+2)$ and get $(+5)$. Then go to the next step $(+5)-(+7)$, using the same method it is changed to $(+5)+(-7)$ and get (-2). Keep doing this way term by term, until we finally finish the whole calculation. As you see, the process is long and tedious. Because there are too many steps it is easy to make an error here or there in the long process. If any step is wrong, you would continue to be wrong step by step until you get the final wrong answer. What a hard and dangerous work it is!

Apply the method of Dr.C, for any long expressions we always have only 3 or 4 steps, only write down 3 or 4 lines. The whole process is therefore greatly simplified.

$$(+3)-(-2)-(+7)+(-1)+(-6)-(+2)+(-3)-(-8)-(+1)$$
$$= 3+2-7-1-6-2-3+8-1$$
$$= (3+2+8)+(-7-1-6-2-3-1)$$
$$= (13)+(-20)$$
$$= -7$$

Here step 1 is to open all brackets. When you open them you apply the "sign times sign" method. To multiply signs is easy. Every student knows how to do it.

The next two steps: We collect all positive numbers and collect all negative numbers. We may skip the third line and directly go from the second line to the fourth line.

Dr.C's method is **not to evaluate term by term**, but to add all positive numbers together and add (collect, sum up) all negative numbers together. Note that for all negative numbers we **add them together**, this makes the job much easier. Still use chess as an analogy, black pieces are 3, 2, 8, together the sum is +13; red pieces are -7, -1, -6, -2, -3 and -1, together we have -20. In this step **we only do addition, no subtraction at all**, that is easy. After this step, there are only one positive number and one negative number left, regardless of the fact how long the original expression was.

In this question we have $(13)+(-20)$, so the answer is -7.

Dr.C's method is easy and short (*always* only three or four lines), tidy and clear (no term to be crossed out) and effective. In the whole process we only add, no subtraction, not many lines to write, and no lengthy consecutive term by term calculations. Hence there is much less chance for the students to make an error. If we divide the class into two groups one uses Dr.C's method, the other uses the traditional method, the difference will be observed immediately. Which method is better, faster, and easier? It is very clear.

Suppose the question is even more complicated like the following:

$$-2(-1) + 3(-1) - 5(+2) + 4(+3) - 6(-1) + 2(-7)$$
$$= 2 - 3 - 10 + 12 + 6 - 14$$
$$= 20 - 27$$
$$= -7$$

Dr.C's method is still the same: **only three steps, only addition**. Positive meets negative only once (at the very end). Step 1 we open all brackets by multiplying signs and numbers, step 2 we sum up, collect all numbers of the same sign (doing addition, not subtraction so it is easy). After two steps we only have one positive number and one negative number left, one more step and the question is done. Plus, minus, multiplication and division mixed operations of integers used to be so hard, and now they become easy. Students enjoy this method. Now they can evaluate 10 terms, 20 terms quickly!

6.2   If $a > b > 0$, which expression is greater?

Mario and Wayne asked Dr.C: "If $a > b > 0$, is a^b greater, or b^a greater? In order to increase the result, which way is more effective, using a larger number risen to a lower exponent, or a smaller number raised to a higher power? If we want to make m^n greater, which way is faster, to increase the base m or to increase the index of exponent n?"

"Good question," said Dr.C. "Analyzing various possibilities certainly increases our knowledge about exponents. Through this study we will understand exponents more deeply. In most cases to increase the power is more efficient. For instance $2^{50} = 1.126 \times 10^{15}$ while $50^2 = 2500$. The difference is so obvious.

"If the base and the index of exponent are close to each other, for example if they only differ by 1, what would be the situation? Please note that $3^2 > 2^3$ but $4^3 < 3^4$. Hence it is reasonable to assume that there exists a number m *between 2 and 3*, such that $m^{m+1} = (m+1)^m$. The approximate solution of this equation is $m = 2.293$, with $2.293^{3.293} = 15.3748$ and $3.293^{2.293} = 15.3758$, very close. From here if we increase the value of m ($m > 2.293$), the exponent would be more important (examples: $3^4 > 4^3$, $4^5 > 5^4$ etc.); if we decrease the value of m ($m < 2.293$), the base will be more important, like $2^3 < 3^2$ or $1^2 < 2^1$."

Dr.C told Mario and Wayne: "Please be more accurate when you do exponential calculations. Because exponential functions are quite sensitive to the changes, we better keep more decimals during the calculation and round off only at the end. The curve of $y = a^x$ is steep when $a > 1$ and $x > 2$. A small change of x may result a big change of y.

"Here is an example, assume that it takes 10 min for the number of bacteria in a bacteria culture to increase exponentially from 350 to 444, then when can the number reach 1000? Let us get the equation $444 = 350a^{10}$, the answer is $a = 1.0240744....$ Next let $1000 = 350(1.0240744)^x$, and the answer is $x = 44$ min. If we round off the value of a to 2 decimals, then

97

the answer of $1000 = 350(1.02)^x$ will be $x = 53$ min. The error here is as high as 20%."

Mario agreed: "Surprising! It is unexpected that the error is so large. Exponents are sensitive. I'll keep more digits during the calculation until I finish it."

Wayne asked another question: "Dr.C, we know that 0^1 is 0, while $1^0 = 1$ and $1^1 = 1$, they are all defined. Why is 0^0 undefined?"

Dr.C laughed: "Well, the 0th power of a number is 1, it comes from the formula $1 = \dfrac{x^n}{x^n} = x^{n-n} = x^0$. The denominator cannot be zero so $x = 0$ is excluded. However, why don't we consider the question in an easier and more relaxed manner? Don't be too serious. (Students laughed). Because the 0th power of 'any' number is 1, and 'any' power of 0 is 0, so we don't know what is 0^0. Should we follow this rule or follow that rule? Should we consider 0^0 as 0 lifted to some power (so that the answer would still be 0), or as a number risen to 0th power (so that the answer would be 1)? We get headache from the two choices. We don't know where to go. We don't want to be self-contradictory and not justified, so what can we do? We simply say that '0 to the power of 0 is undefined'."

Everyone in that class laughed. That successful math class ended in such a cheerful atmosphere.

6.3   Squares and square roots

Dr.C asked the students: "Is it correct to say that the square of a number is greater than the number itself; and the square root of a number is less than the number itself?"

Teddy and Julie replied: "Yes, it is right, $3^2 = 9$, $\sqrt{9} = 3$."

Many students did not agree with them. Donna said: "The square of 1 is 1, the square root of 1 is still 1; not bigger nor smaller."

The class had a heated discussion.. Dr.C encouraged the discussion and wrote down the results on the white board. Further analysis showed the following things:

Squares:

$a^2 = a$	possible (if $a = 0$ or $a = 1$)
$a^2 > a$	possible (if $a < 0$ or $a > 1$)
$a^2 < a$	possible (if $0 < a < 1$, like $0.6^2 = 0.36 < 0.6$)
$a^2 = -a$	possible (if $a = 0$ or $a = -1$)
$a^2 > -a$	possible (if $a > 0$ or $a < -1$. example $a = -2$)
$a^2 < -a$	possible (if $-1 < a < 0$)

Square roots:

$\sqrt{a} = a$	possible (if $a = 0$ or $a = 1$)
$\sqrt{a} > a$	possible (if $0 < a < 1$, example: $\sqrt{0.04} = 0.2$)
$\sqrt{a} < a$	possible (if $a > 1$)
$\sqrt{a} = -a$	possible (if $a = 0$)
$\sqrt{a} > -a$	possible (if $a > 0$)

$\sqrt{a} < -a$ impossible

This time it was impossible. After many times "possible", suddenly came an answer "impossible", making some students not prepared. $\sqrt{a}$ required that $a \geq 0$, therefore $-a \leq 0$. If $a = 0$, $\sqrt{a} = -a$; if $a \neq 0$, then $a > 0$, $\sqrt{a} > -a$.

Dr.C summarized the topic and said: "People accumulate their knowledge during the process of study. The higher you stand the wider horizon your vision can see. At the beginning you might think, the more you add, the greater the sum would be; and the more you subtract the less the result would be. Once you learn negative numbers you know that adding a negative number reduces the answer; subtracting a negative number from a number makes the number greater. As to multiplication and division a beginner might think that multiplication increases a number; and dividing a number by a number decreases that original number. However a number is unchanged when it is multiplied by 1 or divided by 1. Consider a positive number: If it is multiplied by a positive number less than 1, the number decreases. If it is divided by a positive number less than 1 it will increase (like $4 \times 0.1 = 0.4$, $4 \times 0.1 \times 0.1 = 0.04$; whereas $6 \div 0.5 = 12$, $6 \div 0.5 \div 0.5 = 24$)."

Finally Dr.C said: "You may consider more complicated cases, these cases will be more challenging. I suggest you to try them by yourself."

6.4   Math fallacies

Some statements in mathematics sound right, but actually are wrong. Some statements in mathematics sound wrong, but actually are correct. Because we have learned integers, these situations become more obvious.

[1] Dr.C said to his students: "When a large number is multiplied by a large number the result is large. Is this a correct statement? Do you agree with it?"

It sounded right. Everybody knew that bigger number multiplication 8×9, the product is greater than the product of 2×4. However, that statement is *not always true*. Once you learned negative numbers things would change. "For example the number 4 is greater than -6, and 2 is greater than -3 ; the product $4 \times 2 = 8$ is *less* than the product $(-6) \times (-3) = 18$," said Dr.C.

[2] Dr.C continued: "We know that if the numerator of a fraction is increased or the denominator of a fraction is decreased, the value of the fraction increases, such as $\dfrac{5}{9} < \dfrac{7}{9}$ and $\dfrac{7}{9} < \dfrac{7}{8}$. Let me ask you: Is this *always* true?

"Again, no! Although it sounds right, it's not always true. Once negative numbers are allowed, we face other possibilities. (N = the numerator, D = the denominator)

N ↑, D ↓, the fraction is unchanged: $\dfrac{-2}{5} = \dfrac{4}{-10}$

N ↑, D ↓, the fraction is increased: $\dfrac{-2}{5} < \dfrac{1}{-10}$

N ↑, D ↓, the fraction is decreased: $\dfrac{-2}{5} > \dfrac{6}{-10}$ "

[3] "Some people say that it is true when a large number is added to another large number, the sum is greater than the sum of two smaller numbers. Do you agree? Also if a number C is subtracted from A, and the

same C is subtracted from B where $A > B$, then we must have $A - C > B - C$. Do you agree?"

"Well, these two statements are always true regardless of the signs of A, B, and C. They are not fallacies. Since addition and subtraction are different from multiplication, the rule 'negative times negative the result is positive' does not apply to addition and subtraction".

[4] Inspired by Dr.C's examples, the class raised more interesting problems. They knew that sometimes a statement which sounded true might not really be true or might not be *always* true. Jennifer asked: "If a square is cut into two pieces along a straight line and one piece is thrown out, do you think that the piece leftover has less internal angles?"

It might be true, but not always be true. The part leftover might have

three internal angles if you cut along a diagonal so the square became two triangles, each part had 3 angles;

four angles, if you cut the square along a line which passed through only one vertex and ends at the opposite side;

five angles, if you cut a small corner off the square;

as shown in the diagram below.

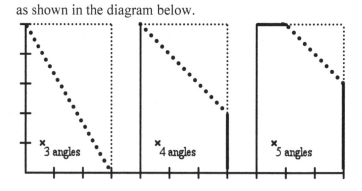

[5]   Here is another question which looks wrong but actually is correct. Ophelia did an investigation and found some interesting results: In her class 1/2 students like to play computer games; 1/6 like to play basketballs; 1/4 like to participate art shows; 1/9 like to read and write poems; and 1/12 like swimming. How many students are there in her class?

Wayne asked: "Is it impossible since $\dfrac{1}{2} + \dfrac{1}{6} + \dfrac{1}{4} + \dfrac{1}{9} + \dfrac{1}{12} > 1$?"

Ophelia replied: "No problem. A person may like to play basketball, to read books and to write poems at the same time. Things here can be overlapped."

Diana said: "Even though, it still seems to be a question without answer. Because the question only has fractions not a single specific number, we do not know 'exactly how many students like sports', etc.

Ophelia smiled: "Be smart. This question looks like unrealistic and impossible, but actually it is realistic and possible."

Yes it is possible, because the number of students must be a natural number, which can be divided by 2, 4, 6, 9, and 12. To be short the number must be divided by 4 and by 9. (If it can be divided by 4, don't worry about 2, etc.) . So the possible number of the students could be 36, 72, 108, etc. However the size of a class is limited, so the most probable answer is 36. You can answer with confidence that Ophelia's class probably has 36 students.

6.5 The fastest way to factor a trinomial

Dr.C discussed factoring with his students. To factor a trinomial $ax^2 + bx + c$, most schools taught the following method: "find two numbers x_1 and x_2 such that $x_1 + x_2 = -\dfrac{b}{a}$ and $x_1 x_2 = \dfrac{c}{a}$, then the original expression can be factored as $ax^2 + bx + c = a(x - x_1)(x - x_2)$."

For example, $x^2 - 5x + 6 = (x - 2)(x - 3)$, because in this question $a = 1$, $b = -5$ and $c = 6$, and $2 + 3 = 5 = -\dfrac{b}{a}$, $2 \times 3 = 6 = \dfrac{c}{a}$.

However, this was a simple question whose answers were clear; a simple look would solve the problem. For more complicated problems like $12x^2 - 7x - 10$, it would be difficult to find two solutions such that $x_1 + x_2 = \dfrac{7}{12}$ and $x_1 x_2 = \dfrac{-10}{12}$. (Answers: $x_1 = \dfrac{5}{4}$ and $x_2 = -\dfrac{2}{3}$).

Dr.C told the students not worry, he introduced a method. He first used $x^2 - 5x + 6 = (x - 2)(x - 3)$ as an example.

"Step 1; write the expression as two empty brackets $x^2 - 5x + 6 = (x \quad)(x \quad)$. In order to get x^2 we use x and x. Step 2; look at the last number （6）. To get 6, there are different ways 2×3 or 1×6. Try the *close pair* (2×3) first. If this pair does not work try another combination 1×6. Step 3; check the sign of the last term. A positive third term (+6) means to use *the same sign* in both brackets, either both positive (+ +) or both negative ($- -$). Now comes the last step: because the sign of the middle term $(-5x)$ is negative, the two signs actually are $- -$. The answer is $x^2 - 5x + 6 = (x-2)(x-3)$.

"If the last term sign is negative, then we get one positive and one negative $(+, -)$ or $(-, +)$. For example $x^2 - x - 6 = (x-3)(x+2)$. Why not $(x+3)(x-2)$? Because that way the middle term would be positive.

"In more complicated cases like $12x^2 - 7x - 10$, we also write down two empty brackets first. To get 12 we may consider $12 = 1 \times 12$, 2×6, or 3×4. Again we start with the *close pair* 3×4 (if not good we will try the next pair 2×6. If it still fails we will consider 1×6. Hence the first step is $12x^2 - 7x - 10 = (3x \quad)(4x \quad)$.

"Because the last term is -10, we try 2 and 5 first (use 10 and 1 as the next choice). The last term is negative so we get one plus sign and one minus sign. The middle term $-7x$ has a negative sign so that the dominant (greater) product should have a $(-)$ sign. The result therefore is $12x^2 - 7x - 10 = (3x+2)(4x-5)$.

"With the method of the next section we can easily check the answer and see that the factoring was done correctly."

6.6   How to check the results of factoring?

Next lesson Dr.C taught the class how to check the results of factoring. He started with the same example of the last section $12x^2 - 7x - 10 = (3x+2)(4x-5)$:

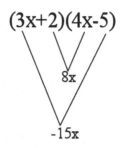

(3x+2)(4x-5)

8x

-15x

"The product of the two middle terms is $+8x$, the product of the outer terms (the first and the last) is $-15x$, together we have $-7x$, exactly what we expected. It equals the middle term of the original expression $-7x$.

"Suppose we write $35x^2 - 37x - 6$ as $(5x + 2)(7x - 3)$, then both the first term $(35x^2)$ and the third term -6 can still be obtained, but the middle term is wrong. According to our method $14x$ and $-15x$ together make $-x$, not the $-37x$ we want. When this occurs we may try to switch the two numbers 2 and 3, if the answer is still incorrect we may try another pair 1 and 6 instead of 2 and 3. If the middle term is only wrong in sign (correct in absolute value) then we only need to switch the two signs. That is, if we write the answer as $(5x + 6)(7x - 1)$, the method of checking will produce $42x - 5x = 37x$, not the original middle term $-37x$. In that case we only need to switch the two signs and get the correct answer $(5x - 6)(7x + 1)$, now $-42x + 5x = -37x$.

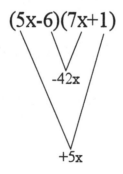

(5x-6)(7x+1)

-42x

+5x

106

"Is this method easy to use? At the first glance it might look not simple. However once you learn it, it will be a very efficient and quick method. Through only 1 or 2 sec you can check a factoring problem. If you do not get the middle term, switch the numbers or try to use another pair. If you get the correct absolute value of the middle term but with a wrong sign, just switch the two signs. It's done!"

6.7 How to decide that a trinomial cannot be factored?

Trinomial $x^2 + x + 1$ cannot be factored. This is not hard to Dr.C's students. However in case we have a more complicated trinomial, it may not be obvious that a given trinomial can or cannot be factored. "I tried already but I could not get it factored," such an excuse is not acceptable.

Today students asked Dr.C: "Can you please teach us how to confirm that a given trinomial $ax^2 + bx + c$ cannot be factored --- absolutely impossible, no one (even you) can do it?"

Dr.C said: "When it is necessary, quickly calculate the value of $\Delta = \sqrt{b^2 - 4ac}$, If Δ is an integer, the trinomial can certainly be factored. If you have not found the answer, work harder, don't stop. For example, the coefficients of $12x^2 - 163x - 70$ are quite large, one may not be able to see how to factor it at once, but $\Delta = \sqrt{b^2 - 4ac} = 173$ is an integer so there *must be* some way to factor it. Under this situation do not give up, continue to try, until you get the correct answer $12x^2 - 163x - 70 = (12x + 5)(x - 14)$."

Dr.C continued: "What happens if Δ is not an integer (example $\Delta = 2.3164$), or it does not exist (example, $\Delta = \sqrt{-6}$)? That means the trinomial is impossible to be factored (see notes below for an exception). For example $6x^2 - 4x - 27$ has coefficients $a = 6$, $b = -4$, and $c = -27$. Its $\Delta = \sqrt{b^2 - 4ac} = \sqrt{664}$ is not an integer, therefore *stop doing it* immediately. Do not waste your time! This method helps us to decide whether a trinomial can or cannot be factored. If it can be factored, continue to try, don't give up. If it is not possible, simply stop immediately!

"What is the exception I mentioned above? Well, if every term of a trinomial has a common factor then pull it out first. For example $2x^2 - 6x - 12$, if you apply my method right now, $2x^2 - 6x - 12$ ($a = 2$, $b = -6$, $c = -12$) would produce a value of Δ not an integer ($\Delta = \sqrt{b^2 - 4ac} = \sqrt{(-6)^2 - 4(2)(-12)} = \sqrt{132}$). However this trinomial can actually be factored one step, $2x^2 - 6x - 12 = 2(x^2 - 3x - 6)$. So we should always check whether there is a common factor of all three terms (like the 2 in this example). If yes, factor it. This is quite easy so it does not affect the usefulness of our method."

"Don't think that a small coefficient trinomial is always easier to be factored than a larger number one. This is sometimes true but not always true." said Dr.C. " $6x^2 - 3x + 1$ cannot be factored because $b^2 - 4ac = 9 - 24 < 0$; whereas $9x^2 - 24x + 7$ (with larger coefficients) can be factored because $b^2 - 4ac = 324$ is a perfect square number (18^2).

"When it is hard to factor, but we do know it *can* be factored (like $7x^2 + 43x - 644$, where $\Delta = \sqrt{b^2 - 4ac} = \sqrt{19881} = 141$ is an integer), we can try the following way to help us factor it. Consider the equation

108

$7x^2 + 43x - 644 = 0$, its two solutions can be found by the quadratic formula

$$x = \frac{-b \pm \sqrt{b^2 - 4ac}}{2a} = \frac{-43 \pm \sqrt{19881}}{2(7)} = 7, \text{ or } -\frac{92}{7}$$

"Therefore $7x^2 + 43x - 644 = (7x + 92)(x - 7)$. At first this method seems to take some time, but actually it is fast enough for large coefficient trinomials."

Through this lesson students of Dr.C learned a method. Now when they see a hard factoring question, they quickly apply this method first to check whether the result is "yes" or "no". If the result is "yes, it can be factored", then work hard until the answer is found. If the result is "no, it cannot be factored", then do not waste time, stop immediately.

Chapter 7
Algebra and Linear Equation

7.1   Fundamental philosophy of algebra

Dr.C discussed a question with math teachers: "What is the fundamental philosophy of algebra?" They all agreed that as teachers they should not only teach the students how to calculate, but also help the students to master the basic philosophy behind the numbers and symbols. Therefore to know the fundamental idea of algebra is important.

Naturally, the next question would be: "What is the fundamental philosophy of algebra?"

Dr.C said: "My point of view is that, algebra replaces hundreds or thousands things by one symbol, one quantity. View many things as one, so that the problems can be greatly simplified."

"For example, a student may know how to evaluate $2a+3a$, but may not know how to evaluate or simplify a long expression like $2(3x^2y-4xy^3+y^4-10x^5y^{-7})+3(3x^2y-4xy^3+y^4-10x^5y^{-7})$.

"This is because he or she has not learned how to view the long expression in the brackets just as a single quantity, or a single 'apple', and hence does not know that the long question is actually simple --- two apples plus three apples."

"Even if the expression is more complicated, like

$$u^{-3}v^8 + 2(3x^2y - 4xy^3 + y^4 - 10x^5y^{-7}) - 6c^{-9}$$
$$+3(3x^2y - 4xy^3 + y^4 - 10x^5y^{-7}) + 4u^{-3}v^8 - 24c^{-9}$$

"It is just another simple question of 'two apples plus three apples, one banana plus four bananas', where we view $u^{-3}v^8 - 6c^{-9}$ as a banana.

"Once we are used to this kind of view (to view many terms as a single symbol), our ability to handle algebraic questions is raised to a new level. In our eyes there are no longer lots of complicated incomprehensible mess, instead, we see clear rules, reasonable combinations and organized items.

"Thus, when we calculate $\left(\dfrac{3p^5n^6}{m^4} - \dfrac{8p^2n^9}{m^7} \right)^3$, do not panic. See it as a simple question $(a-b)^3$, apply the expansion formula $(a-b)^3 = a^3 - 3a^2b + 3ab^2 - b^3$ to expand it. Otherwise one might calculate the cube by multiplying the long expression by itself and by itself again. Only when we understand the fundamental philosophy of algebra, do we understand the great power of mathematics."

7.2 Correcting common mistakes of students

"To give a man a fish is not as effective as teaching him how to fish." Most times Dr.C does not point out the mistakes of the students directly; instead, he often tries to guide the students to learn from their own experience.

Today Dr.C used his method, discussed possible mistakes made by the students during the study of algebra.

[Mistake 1: Evaluating $a^6b + a^6b$ as $a^{12}b^2$]

Victor evaluated $a^6b + a^6b$ as $a^{12}b^2$. Dr.C did not point out the mistake; instead he invited Victor to do another question $a^6b \times a^6b$. When Victor got the same result $a^{12}b^2$, he immediately realized that he was wrong in doing the first question.

Then, Dr.C asked Victor "Adding one apple to one apple already on the table, how many apples are there?" The answer of course should be two apples. Dr.C continued: "In doing $a^6b + a^6b$, just consider a^6b as *an apple*, therefore the correct answer should be $a^6b + a^6b = 2a^6b$. We should build a habit to treat a long algebraic expression as 'one apple', ignore the inside structure."

[Mistake 2: Doing $(a+b)^{10}$ as $a^{10} + b^{10}$]

Jenny calculated $(a+b)^{10}$ as $a^{10} + b^{10}$ and she did not realize that was a mistake. Instead of telling her that was wrong, Dr.C invited her to evaluate $(3+1)^2$ (answer 16); and $3^2 + 1^2$ (answer 10) respectively. Since the answers were different Jenny immediately realized that something was wrong in her original calculation. Indeed $(a+b)^n \neq a^n + b^n$ for $n \neq 1$.

[Mistake 3: Treating $\sqrt{a^2 - b^2}$ as $a - b$]

This, and similar mistakes, like doing $\sqrt[3]{a^3 + b^3}$ as $a + b$, doing $\sin(A + B)$ as $\sin A + \sin B$, etc., were found in many student's homework.

Dr.C told the students a non-linear relation should not be done this way, for example $3-1=2$ but $\sqrt{3^2-1^2}=\sqrt{9-1}=\sqrt{8}=2\sqrt{2}$. Non-linear calculations like the square, square root, trigonometric functions, logarithms, exponents, etc., should not be done this way in general. Under special cases we might have exceptions. For example in general $(a+b)^2 \neq a^2+b^2$. However if one of the two was 0 then we have $(a+0)^2=a^2+0^2$.

[Mistake 4: Repeated multiplications]

Michael calculated $(4)(2)(3x^2+5y)$ and he got $8(12x^2+20y)$, it was wrong, he multiplied 4 to 2 *and* to $(3x^2+5y)$. Dr.C showed him one example: $4\times3\times2=12\times2=24$, but $4\times3\times2 \neq (4\times3)(4\times2)$.

[Mistake 5: Forgot unit conversion]

Such as writing the total value $2.85 of x dimes and y quarters as $10x+25y=2.85$, the correct way should be either (in cents) $10x+25y=285$ or (in dollars) $0.10x+0.25y=2.85$.

Other mistakes in solving equations included the error to move a term from one side to the other side of an equation without changing the sign, to get rid of the denominator of a rational equation by only multiplying the common denominator to one side of the equation, or simply to write down $-3(5-2x)$ as $-15-6x$, instead of the correct answer $-15+6x$.

The students learned math from their own mistakes.

7.3 Should synthetic division use addition or subtraction?

Jessica and friends are learning polynomial division from their school. There are two ways to do division in algebra: long division and synthetic division. For questions like $(3x^3 - 2x^2 + 5x - 1) \div (x - 4)$, both ways are applicable but it is simpler to do the synthetic division. However, different teachers may teach different methods to do the same division question; some prefer addition, others use subtraction.

Using the above example, we may write -4 outside, and apply subtraction (the first line minus the second line):

$$
\begin{array}{r|rrrr}
 & 3 & -2 & 5 & -1 \\
-4 & \downarrow & -12 & -40 & -180 \quad \text{(subtraction)} \\
\hline
 & 3 & 10 & 45 & 179
\end{array}
$$

Here the number 3 moves down to the bottom line, $-4 \times 3 = -12$, then $(-2) - (-12) = 10$, etc. The final result is $3x^2 + 10x + 45$, with remainder 179.

Equivalently we may also write 4 (not -4) outside, and use addition (the top line plus the second line):

$$
\begin{array}{r|rrrr}
 & 3 & -2 & 5 & -1 \\
4 & \downarrow & 12 & 40 & 180 \quad \text{(addition)} \\
\hline
 & 3 & 10 & 45 & 179
\end{array}
$$

Here the number 3 again moves down to the bottom line $4 \times 3 = 12$, then $(-2) + (12) = 10$, etc. The final result is the same as above, $3x^2 + 10x + 45$ with the remainder 179.

Dr.C asks the class to vote, in order to see which method is more welcomed by the students. The results show that more students prefer the way with addition because addition makes fewer mistakes than subtraction. Another reason is that when we apply the remainder theorem to find the remainder of the above question, we use 4, not −4 so $f(4) = 3(4^3) - 2(4^2) + 5(4) - 1 = 179$ is the remainder. Nevertheless some students still like the way with subtraction. Their reason is that when we do ordinary division (a number divided by another number, such as $1135 \div 6$), we use subtraction step by step.

Jessica asks: "Now that when we do division we know the remainder, why do we still need to learn the remainder theorem?"

Dr.C invites Jessica and other students to find the remainder of $(x^{99} - 1) \div (x + 1)$ by division. They realize that to do such a question we need to *insert 98 zeroes* between x^{99} and 1. Now they fully understand the reason.

When both the long division and the synthetic division are applicable, synthetic division is simpler. Because in synthetic division we only input the coefficients, not the x terms (for example $-2x^2$ is written as -2). There is another advantage: We only need to write three rows when we do synthetic division, instead of writing the formula row by row again and again. However, questions like $f(x) \div (2x^3 - 5x + 1)$ cannot be done by synthetic division, they can only be evaluated by long division. Usually the method of synthetic division is applicable to questions where the divisor is a

116

linear relation, i.e., when $f(x)$ is divided by either $(x-a)$, or divided by $(ax-b)$ (which is equivalent to $\div(x-\frac{b}{a})$ first, then $\div a$). Therefore, $f(x)\div(x^2-x-42)$ can be done by synthetic division because (x^2-x-42) can be factored so that we can divide the original function $f(x)$ by $(x-7)$ then by $(x+6)$ or in reversed order. Unlike this, the question $f(x)\div(2x^3-5x+1)$ can only be done by long division because the divisor cannot be factored.

7.4   Converting algebraic problems from hard to easy

Barbie is a young math teacher. One day she asked Dr.C, "How can I help my students easily solve advanced algebraic problems?"

Dr.C replied: "There are many methods to convert from hard to easy. Let us study a question: 'How many integers are there between 1677 and 4132 inclusive?' Of course we should not count numbers one by one. If we subtract 1677 from 4132, that is still wrong. Why? We may ask the students a much simpler question first: 'how many integers are there between 2 and 5 inclusive?' The answer is 4 (four numbers 2, 3, 4, 5). Since $5-2=3$, we know that we need to add 1 after the subtraction. Therefore from 1677 to 4132 inclusive, we do subtraction $4132-1677=2455$ first then add 1 to the answer. The answer is 2456. In this example we use a similar structure but much simpler question to teach the students the method.

"If we want to know how many integers are there between −734 and **4907** inclusive, we may divide it into three parts: negative (

$-1, -2, \ldots -734$), zero, and positive (1 to 4907), then it is not hard. Equivalently we may calculate $4907 - (-734) + 1$ and get the same answer.

"A beginner may have difficulty to solve the algebraic equation $28.795 = \dfrac{0.4652}{x - 1.1386}$. Well, we may ask the student to solve a similar but easier equation $3 = \dfrac{6}{x}$ instead. The answer $x = 2$ is obvious because $6 \div 2 = 3$. An analogy to the way we solve this simple problem is to change the original equation to $x - 1.1386 = \dfrac{0.4652}{28.795}$, therefore $x - 1.1386 = 0.0162$ and $x = 1.1548$.

"If a student does not know how to solve an equation $921.67x + 129.77 = 316.44$, we may ask her or him to solve a simpler but similar structure equation $2x + 1 = 3$ first, then apply the same strategy to solve the original long equation. The advantage is, when the number is so small, it is easy to see directly what should be the answer and what should be the correct way to solve that problem. Now go back to the long equation and we will not be afraid of the larger numbers."

Finally Dr.C said: "If we compare the task to *write* an equation in a word problem with the task to *solve* that equation, then the former is more important. One day I gave my students 100 word problems and asked them just to write down the equations without solving them. I told the students that I believe that they were able to solve the equations algebraically. I only wanted to see the 100 equations, not the 100 solutions. Under that kind of training my students improved their ability effectively."

Barbie listened carefully and understood Dr.C's method, her confidence to teach mathematics increased after the conversation.

7.5   We may be smarter than our calculators

Pam, a student of Dr.C, bought a new calculator. Compared to the calculator of Dr.C, Pam found that hers was much more advanced and more expensive. Pam therefore asked Dr.C `Why don't you buy a better calculator?"

Dr.C answered with a smile: "When I was a high school student no one in my class ever had a calculator, every calculation was done by hands and brain, plus a printed table (a chart) of mathematics. Due to that reason, today my ability of mental math is better than yours. When I was a child my mother taught me math strictly. When I made a mistake she did not allow me to use an eraser, often I had to re-write the whole page again. My first calculator came to me when I was at my 30s, and of course that was a very simple one.

"If you study the history of great mathematicians like Gauss, Euler, Lagrange, none of them even had a chance to see a modern calculator. However, they did great work on mathematics, derived many classical theorems, and calculated the orbits of many planets and stars. Their work shines forever. Without calculators our calculation ability is not as good as those great masters of mathematics.

"In today's world where every child will use a calculator earlier or later, it may not be a good idea to use calculators too early or too often. A child depending on calculators too much might not be able to evaluate a simple question (like $7 \div 2$) without a calculator. If a person meets a simple question and always tries to use a calculator, this person may forget how to do addition, subtraction, multiplication and division mentally. You can see that the difference of the ability to learn mathematics starts from here. We have all heard of people who use computer word processor skillfully but once they have to use a pen to write, they make many errors, forget the spelling of many words.

"A music written by Mozart several hundred years ago can still be recognized by today's musicians, while a music recorded by technology onto a phonogram record or an audio cassette tape may not be played nowadays because newer CD players do not recognize music recorded by those 'out of date' methods, and CDs themselves are replaced by newer technology these days. Technology develops fast and is out of date very frequently. So I hope you do not ignore the fundamental ways to calculate by hand and brain.

"Some questions may be easy for us but hard for a calculator. Don't believe it? For example, is **9305420713580940682** a perfect square number? Too many digits make it impossible for an ordinary calculator to calculate and display the results. However, we know from our experience that if a whole number ends with 0, 1, 2, 8, 9, its square ends with 0, 1, 4. If a number ends with 3, 4, 5, 6, 7, its square ends with 9, 6, 5. Therefore the square of a whole number cannot end with a 2 (or 3, 7, 8). Note, my friends, this kind of problem has a feature: **it is easy to say no, but hard to say yes**. For example if a number ends with 9, we don't have a sure answer, (example: $169 = 13^2$, but 179 is not the square of a whole number). If a number ends with 3, we know it cannot be the square of a whole number. If a number ends with 9, we do not have a certain conclusion."

Dr.C continued: "Sometimes it is our human error when we use a calculator but get a wrong answer. For example if we want to find the mean value of 6, 18 and 87, we should add them together then divide the answer by 3. If we press 6 + 18 + 87 ÷ 3 on a calculator, then we get the wrong answer 53. The correct way is to press the equal sign key after we add the three numbers and *before* we do the division. Otherwise the calculator would automatically perform the division first (following the order of operations), and you are actually doing $6+18+(87 \div 3) = 6+18+29 = 53$. Even high school students are prone to make this type of mistakes. In order to apply the quadratic formula to solve a quadratic equation $ax^2 + bx + c = 0$, the formula is $x = \dfrac{-b \pm \sqrt{b^2 - 4ac}}{2a}$. Using a calculator to apply this formula we must remember to press the equal sign key once we finish the top part. If your calculator accepts the formulas input, do not forget to include the necessary brackets."

Julie asked: "How can we know the speed of a calculator?" Dr.C replied: "Let two calculators do a long question such as to evaluate $69!$, or repeat additions like 3+3+3+3+3+3 in a fast way, if the answer on one calculator is wrong, that calculator does not work fast enough."

7.6   A young kid "proves" that "1413 = 1376"

Today the students of Dr.C were quite enthusiastic and active. Jay, with the nickname "*smart boy*", showed a math magic to "prove that 1413 = 1376".

Jay first wrote the following on the board:
"Assume that $a - b - c + d - e + f = g - h$

Therefore $37(a - b - c + d - e + f) = 37(g - h)$

$1413(a - b - c + d - e + f) - 1376(a - b - c + d - e + f)$
$= 1413(g - h) - 1376(g - h)$

Move terms:

$$1413(a - b - c + d - e + f) - 1413(g - h)$$
$$= 1376(a - b - c + d - e + f) - 1376(g - h)$$

Hence
$$1413(a - b - c + d - e + f - g + h)$$
$$= 1376(a - b - c + d - e + f - g + h)$$

Divide by $(a - b - c + d - e + f - g + h)$ on both sides, we get $1413 = 1376$."

The result was bizarre and incorrect. How could 1413 equal 1376? Each line seemed right. The students thought: "Oh, there must be something wrong, but the expressions are so long and it is hard to find the error."

At the end they realized that, every step was correct *except* the last one. Because Jay assumed that $a - b - c + d - e + f = g - h$, so the value of the expression $(a - b - c + d - e + f - g + h)$ was zero. Frances said: "We cannot divide an expression by 0, that would lead us to wrong conclusions $1413 \times 0 = 1376 \times 0$ is correct because $0 = 0$, but 1413 is not equal to 1376."

Because Jay's expression was long and the numbers were large, it was hard to find such a hidden mistake. Through this process the students learned something --- "do not be confused by long and tedious expressions."

7.7   Solving magic triangle related questions

Time flies! Summer vacation is near. After several months of hard work, Dr.C thinks it is time to give the students a break, give them some easier and more interesting work to do. He draws the following diagram on the board and asks the students: "How can you place the numbers 1 to 6 into the circles so that every side of the triangle adds up to the same sum? Remember, there may be more than one way to do it."

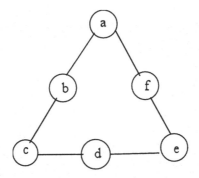

This question is not hard; Erika and Thomas get the answers by different methods. Thomas applies algebra; he assigns letters a, b, c, d, e, f to the six empty positions and writes:

$$a + b + c = k$$
$$a + f + e = k$$
$$c + d + e = k$$

Here k is the magic number (the sum of the three numbers along any side). Add the three equations:

$$(a + b + c + d + e + f) + (a + c + e) = 3k$$

Note that $(a + b + c + d + e + f) = 21$. We are not saying that $a = 1$, $b = 2$, etc.; instead we merely state that under whatever order the sum $(a + b + c + d + e + f)$ is *always* equal to the sum $1 + 2 + 3 + 4 + 5 + 6 = 21$. Therefore $21 + (a + c + e) = 3k$, so that

$(a + c + e) = 3k - 21 = 3(k - 7)$. What is the conclusion? It states that the sum of the three *corners* $(a + c + e)$ must be a multiple of 3.

Pick three numbers from 1, 2, 3, 4, 5, 6 to make the sum a multiple of 3, then place the three numbers onto the three corners, the rest is easy. A magic triangle is done this way.

Erika's method is even simpler. She explains: "It can be noticed that not all six empty positions are of equal importance in this question. Obviously the three corners are more important because each of them stays on two lines. The three corner numbers then must have some *special features*: they are either the larger ones (4, 5, 6); or the smaller ones (1, 2, 3); or the odd ones (1, 3, 5); or the even ones (2, 4, 6). Thus we have four ways to construct a magic triangle. Once the four corners are given, it is easy to complete the question. If a line already has two large numbers then insert a small number on that line, and vice versa."

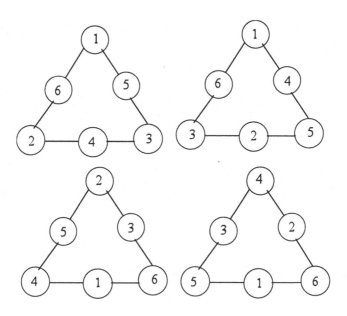

Similarly, if we want to input 1, 2, 3, 4, 5, 6, 7 into the following Y-type diagram, we can apply Erika's method. Among the seven positions only one is special --- the center. Among the seven given numbers which numbers are special? The answers are the smallest one (1), the middle one (4), and the largest one (7). Therefore this question has three solutions, shown below.

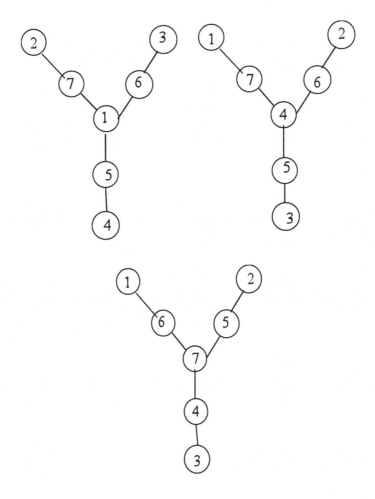

"Good," says Dr.C. "In magic square or magic triangle related problems some points are more important than others. The numbers on those special locations should possess some common features. Numbers there may be the smallest, the greatest, the middle, all even, or all odd. Realizing this will help us solve such questions in an easier and more reasonable way. Later we are going to discuss the most interesting ancient topic of mathematics --- magic squares."

Appendix
Magic Squares

A. Odd order magic squares

What a wonderful topic it is! The classroom is filled with girls and boys from various grades. Everyone loves magic squares! Dr.C says: "People have been interested in magic squares for thousands of years. Our ancestors developed many smart ways to construct various type magic squares. Today let me introduce the fast ways created by our ancestors to make odd order magic squares."

Using a 3×3 magic square as an example, a good method is to list nine consecutive whole numbers in a row, place the middle one into the center location of a 3×3 grid. If the center is an odd number then place the even numbers in z-pattern to the four corners; if the center is an even number place the odd numbers in z-pattern to the four corners. Example: If we use the numbers 0, 1, 2, 3, 4, 5, 6, 7, 8, the middle one (4, an even number) will be placed at the center. Then we place the odd numbers 1, 3, 5, 7 to the four corners so that:

1		3
	4	
5		7

"The sum of the numbers along either diagonal is 12 ($1 + 4 + 7 = 12$, $3 + 4 + 5 = 12$). It is *the* magic number. The top row already has 1 and 3, in order to get 12; we need to place 8 there. Follow this way we can finish the whole magic square quickly."

The process is fast. However, Dr.C says there is an even faster way. It is so simple that *no calculation* is needed. No addition, no subtraction, a magic square is done before we realize what should be its magic number! Even a young kid in grade 1 can do it easily.

"Draw extra squares in each of the four directions (see the diagram below). Starting from any *extra* square, go along one diagonal and place numbers consecutively, we have the following results:

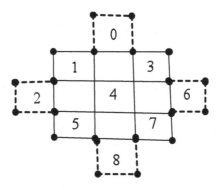

"Now *push* numbers outside the 3×3 region into the original square. Because this is a 3×3 magic square, push each external number three steps into the square. If a number is on top we push it down three steps, if a number is below the square we push it up three steps. If a number is on the left outside we push it right three steps, and if a number is on the right outside we push it left three steps into the central region. (Thus, in this question 0 goes down three steps, 2 moves right three steps, 6 moves left three steps and 8 moves up three steps). We now have the following 3×3 magic square.

1	8	3
6	4	2
5	0	7

"How can we use nine consecutive numbers (for example 1 to 9) to make a 3×3 square such that every line (row, column, diagonal) has a *different* sum of numbers?" asked Dr.C. "Of course you may simply close your eyes and put in the numbers randomly. There is a good chance that you will win because there are many ways to make such a 'counter-magic square'. However, let me tell you a systematic way which is easy to remember and easy to use. Just write down the first number in the center cell and wrap out (or in one corner cell and wrap in), a counter-magic square is there!"

wrap in

1	2	3
8	9	4
7	6	5

wrap out

9	8	7
2	1	6
3	4	5

The next diagram shows a 7×7 magic square. The numbers used are 61, 60, 59, etc. When the order of the magic square is high, the advantage of this method is even more remarkable. In the diagram some numbers are already inside the box, we only need to push each external number 7 steps into the square. For example move the number 57 right 7 steps to the new position (below 40, right of 39). To make the diagram clear only part of the numbers are shown.

All odd order magic squares can be done this way. For example a 11×11 magic square has 121 numbers. If you do not know this method, it is impossible to solve the magic square even if you spend many days on it. Draw one 11×11 square with extra cells on each of the four sides. Input numbers one after another along any one diagonal direction, starting from an external vertex. After that half of the numbers are in good positions and the other half are outside the square. Push each outside number 11 steps into the square and the work is done. It is easy to check that the result is a magic square. Note that we do not know the magic number until we finish the whole work --- there is no addition or subtraction in the whole process. (The following diagram shows how to make a 7×7 magic square.)

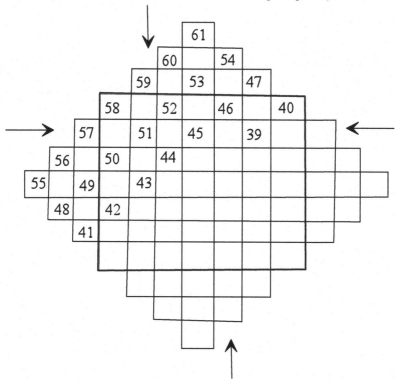

B.   Double even order magic squares

The double even order (4×4, 8×8 etc.) magic squares can be done in various ways. The simplest one is as follows.

Example, use numbers 1 to 16 to make a **4×4** magic square. On a **4×4** grid imagine that you draw two diagonals to divide the 16 cells into two halves. 8 cells have a line passing through (we call them "good cells"), 8 cells do not have a line passing through (we call them "bad cells"). Then input numbers 1 to 16 consecutively into the cells.   In the following diagram if the cell is a good cell, we write the number in it (1, 4, 6, 7, 10, 11, 13, and 16); if the cell is a bad cell, do not put in the number, just *count and pass* it. Now we have:

Count 1 to 16 this way →

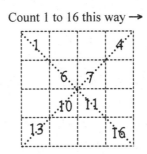

"Good cells" are good; they already have the correct numbers and do not need to be revised later. "Bad cells" need to be re-located. Next, count 1 to 16 again but this time starting from the end position (the bottom right) going backwards. Only place numbers into the empty (bad) positions (shown as smaller numbers). The good cells are already occupied so we just *count and pass* them; do not write anything on them.

1.	15	14	**4**
12	**6.**	**7**	9
8	**10**	**11.**	5
13	3	2	**16.**

Count 1 to 16 backwards this way

←

Believe it or not, you already have a correct **4×4** magic square! No addition, no subtraction. Until you finish the magic square you have no idea what the magic number is! To know the magic number we need to add numbers along a row, a column, or a diagonal.

To make a **8×8** large size magic square we use diagonals to divide the 64 cells into two parts: 32 good cells and 32 bad cells (see the following diagram). Then we do the same as in the **4×4** case. Assume that we use numbers 1 to 64. This method works for any other 64 consecutive whole numbers like 0 to 63, 9 to 72; or 98 to 35, etc. Input number 1 in the first cell, then count one by one but only write down numbers into the good cells (numbers shown without brackets), ignoring the bad cells (count and pass, do not input). When you finish, starting from the end cell count backwards 1,2,3,... but only write numbers into the empty (bad) cells (numbers shown in brackets). When this is done, the whole work is done. In order to be clear we do not show all numbers in the diagram.

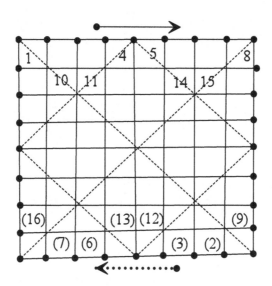

Part 2

(For high school and up)

Chapter 8
System of Equations
Equations of Lines

8.1 Why do we teach Cramer's Rule?

Summer is over, autumn arrives. It's getting cooler. Students are back to schools. Some of them left junior school and became high school students. They are learning to solve coupled linear equations in school.

The methods taught in schools usually contain solving equations by graph, substitution, and elimination. This semester Dr.C added "solving coupled linear equations by determinates --- the Cramer's rule" to his curriculum.

Why?

Dr.C explained the reason in today's class: "First, this method is not hard; it only requires the students to know basic algebra. To know more methods helps you broaden your horizon, review what you have learned and prepare you for future studies including vectors and linear algebra.

"More than that, this method has its own special significance. Whether you use substitution or elimination, there are some decisions that *you* have to make. Substitution and elimination contain human factors, require human decisions.   For example when we solve equations

$\begin{cases} 2x - 3y = 5 \\ x - 7y = -3 \end{cases}$, if we use substitution method we tell ourselves that it is better to start with the second equation (change it to $x = 7y - 3$), otherwise if we try to solve x or y from the first equation we will inevitably face fractions. If we use elimination, we tell ourselves that it is better for us to multiply the second equation by 2 then subtract one equation from the other, or in a more complicated manner we may multiply the first equation by 7 and multiply the second equation by 3, then do a subtraction. Where to start, what number to multiply, adding or subtracting equations, all these are decided *by you*! These artificial decisions may differ from problem to problem.

"However, when we use the Cramer's rule to solve linear equations, the procedure is fixed. You don't need to choose or make any decision when solving the equations. There exists a completely fixed set of formats and algorithm. To solve $\begin{cases} ax + by = c \\ dx + ey = f \end{cases}$, we calculate $D = \det \begin{vmatrix} a & b \\ d & e \end{vmatrix}$,

$D_x = \det \begin{vmatrix} c & b \\ f & e \end{vmatrix}$, $D_y = \det \begin{vmatrix} a & c \\ d & f \end{vmatrix}$; then if $D \neq 0$, we have $x = \dfrac{D_x}{D}$ and

$y = \dfrac{D_y}{D}$. The method to solve three equations is similar. In the process there is no room and no need for human decision. What is the advantage of this feature? It is **good for computers to solve equations**. Because every step is so systematic, no human choice involved, it becomes *the method* for computers to solve coupled linear equations. Once you write a program, for each problem you just need to input the given coefficients (a, b, c, d, e, f) then press a button and the results come! If $D \neq 0$ there is unique set of answers. If $D = D_x = D_y = 0$, there are infinite groups of solutions. (That does not mean any x and y are acceptable, the solution is a straight line in 2-D, not the whole plane). If $D = 0$ but D_x or D_y is not 0, then the given equations have no solution. Similar situation exists for sets of 3-D questions."

Students expressed great interest; they welcomed the new method. Once they learned that the Cramer's rule could be applied to solve coupled linear equations by computers, they showed enormous enthusiasm to write their own programs and to apply their programs to solve sets of equations. They were very happy.

8.2 A tip to avoid sign errors

To apply Cramer's rule requires the students to know how to evaluate determinates. For 2-D that is simple, $\det \begin{vmatrix} a & b \\ c & d \end{vmatrix} = ad - bc$. How can we evaluate a 3-D determinate? University linear algebra textbooks teach students to expand a determinate according to a row or a column (for details of this method, please refer to any university linear algebra textbook). The advantage of expansion is that it works not only for 2-D and 3-D, but also for higher order, n-D determinates.

There is another way to evaluate a 3-D determinate. Although this method does not apply to 4-D or higher order determinates, for 3-D it is easy and convenient. We can expand a 3-D determinate along its diagonals. For example:

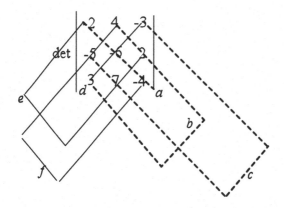

To apply this method it is easy to make an error on the positive sign or the negative sign of each term. Because each line contains the product of three positive or negative numbers and for each of the solid line diagonal products (the lines d, e, f in the diagram; for example the line f is $(4)\times(-5)\times(-4) = 80$) we need to change its sign (change f into $-((4)\times(-5)\times(-4)) = -80$ instead of 80); while no change to the dashed line products (lines a, b, c) .

In order to help the students avoid sign mistakes, Dr.C suggests a simple way: write down three + signs and three − signs in front of the **empty** brackets *before* you input any number, so the above step becomes: (The six numbers below are the products along the lines a, b, c, d, e, and f)

$$= +(\ ) +(\ ) +(\ ) -(\ ) -(\ ) -(\ )$$
$$= (-48)+(24)+(105)-(54)-(-28)-(80)$$
$$= -48 + 24 + 105 - 54 + 28 - 80$$
$$= 157 - 182$$
$$= -25$$

Writing down signs while the brackets are still empty helps us reduce possible confusion about the signs. After that we apply the method introduced in Chapter 6; open the brackets, collect all positive numbers and collect (*add*) all negative numbers, until we only have one positive number and one negative number left.

This diagonal expansion method not only applies to the calculation of 3×3 determinates, it can also be used to evaluate the vector products of 3-D vectors. For example, if vectors $\vec{a} = [2, -1, -3]$ and $\vec{b} = [4, 5, -2]$, we have

$$\vec{a} \times \vec{b} = \begin{vmatrix} \hat{i} & \hat{j} & \hat{k} \\ 2 & -1 & -3 \\ 4 & 5 & -2 \end{vmatrix}$$

$$= (\ ) + (\ ) + (\ ) - (\ ) - (\ ) - (\ )$$
$$= (2\hat{i}) + (-12\hat{j}) + (10\hat{k}) - (-4\hat{k}) - (-15\hat{i}) - (-4\hat{j})$$
$$= 2\hat{i} - 12\hat{j} + 10\hat{k} + 4\hat{k} + 15\hat{i} + 4\hat{j}$$
$$= 17\hat{i} - 8\hat{j} + 14\hat{k}$$

This is similar to the calculation of determinates. Again a small tip (to **write down signs in front of empty brackets first**) helps the students to avoid confusion of signs.

8.3   From the mid-point to an end point

It is well known how to use the formula $(\overline{x}, \overline{y}) = \left(\dfrac{x_1 + x_2}{2}, \dfrac{y_1 + y_2}{2} \right)$ to find the location of the mid-point of two given points. If one end point and the mid-point are given we can apply the same formula to solve equations, calculate the coordinates of the other end point. This can be found in many textbooks, but is it really the easiest method?

Dr.C does not think so. Today he says: "We have a better method. The fundamental idea of our method lies in the fact that the two coordinates x and y are independent to each other. In order to find the y coordinates we can completely ignore the x; similarly to find the x we can completely ignore the y."

"Please study the following example," says Dr.C. "If one end of a line segment AB is $A(1,2)$, and the mid-point of this line segment is $M(-3,5)$, where is the other end B? According to the textbooks we should solve the equations $(-3,5) = \left(\dfrac{1+x_2}{2}, \dfrac{2+y_2}{2} \right)$. This is correct. However, there is an easier way. First, let us forget y, only consider the coordinate x. One end is 1 and the mid-point is -3, like in the following diagram:

$$\overset{\displaystyle ?\qquad\qquad -3\qquad\qquad 1}{\bullet\!-\!\bullet\!-\!\bullet\!-\!\bullet\!-\!\bullet\!-\!\bullet\!-\!\bullet\!-\!\bullet\!-\!\bullet}\ \ \mathbf{x}$$

"From 1 to -3, the number goes down 4 steps. Continue to go down another 4 steps we will arrive at -7, therefore $x_2 = -7$. Similarly for y one end is 2 and the mid-point is 5. From 2 to 5 the number goes up by 3. Continue to go up another 3 steps from 5 the new location is 8, therefore $y_2 = 8$. Hence the other end is $B\ (-7,8)$. Note that we completely ignore one coordinate while we calculate the other coordinate, so our method is easy.

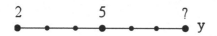

140

"No coupled equations to solve, no fractions to deal with, no lengthy calculations, everything is simple and intuitive. When we discuss x we do not look at y and vice versa. Our method not only simplifies the calculation, but also contains a deep logic, a deep philosophy in it. The philosophy is: the two coordinates of a point are independent to each other."

Dr.C's students welcome this easy method. Even a student who has not learned how to solve equations can find the correct answer, since she or he just needs to count steps.

8.4 Looking for good points to sketch a straight line

To sketch a straight line when its equation is given sounds easy. Today Dr.C asked the students to sketch the graph of the line $4x - 7y = 21$. Scott first changed the equation into the slope and y-intercept form $y = \frac{4}{7}x - 3$, then starting from the y intercept $(0, -3)$, found the next point $(7, 1)$ from the slope (right 7, up 4). Connecting the two points he got the line correctly.

Jacob used another approach. He did not use the slope, but found two points directly. When $x = 1$, $y = \frac{4}{7} - 3 = -\frac{17}{7} \approx -2.4$, so he got one point $(1, -2.4)$. Similarly for $x = 2$, he found another point $(2, -1.9)$. He connected the two points to got the line. Jacob was not happy about the two points he found because he got decimals, not accurate and not convenient to sketch.

141

Students asked Dr.C whether there was a better method. Dr.C said: "Let us use the y-intercept $(0, -3)$ as the first point to start with. Although two points are enough to decide a straight line, three points are better for beginners. If the three points form a broken line (not a straight line), you immediately realize that something must already be wrong. If you sketch a line from only two points and one of the two points is wrong, you still get a straight line but it is not the line you want.

"How can we find a good second point with integer co-ordinates? Let me tell you a tip: **'to find x look at y; to find y look at x'**. What does this mean? Let's use the above example. To sketch the straight line $4x - 7y = 21$, first substitute $x = 0$ and get $y = -3$ so we have the first point $(0, -3)$. Watch carefully what I am going to do: In order to find the x coordinate of the second point, I do not look at the x term of the equation ($4x$), instead I pay attention to the y coefficient of the equation (-7). Hence the next x is either 7 steps up or 7 steps down from the first x value 0. Let $x = 7$ in the equation we have $y = 1$; let $x = -7$ in the equation we get $y = -7$. Therefore the next good point can be either $(7, 1)$ or $(-7, -7)$. This method guarantees that you will get good points without a decimal or fraction.

"If we start with the y-intercept $(0, -3)$ and try to find the y-coordinate of the next good point, look at the x coefficient of the equation $4x - 7y = 21$ (it is a 4). So the next good y value is either $(-3 + 4)$ or $(-3 - 4)$, i.e., either 1 or -7, Using these y values we will certainly get good x values from the equation, no fraction, no decimal. The rule is: *to find x don't look at x, instead look at y; to find y don't look at y, instead look at x.*"

Finally Dr.C said: "Sometimes we need to do the opposite thing, to find the equation of a line from the graph of a line. To do that, we choose two points from the line and calculate the slope $m = \dfrac{y_2 - y_1}{x_2 - x_1}$. These two points are better chosen far from each other to reduce the error during reading or measuring the coordinates. If possible, we better choose points with integer coordinates to simplify the calculation and reduce the error. You see, there are many small tips in the world. Applying these tips we can do our job faster and better.

Chapter 9
Quadratic Equations

9.1 Three ways to solve a quadratic equation

Several students learning math in Dr.C's learning center met together to discuss the ways to solve quadratic equations. Tom said: "I like the method of factoring. It is the fastest and easiest way to solve a quadratic equation. If we want to solve $x^2 - x - 42 = 0$, simply factor it as $(x - 7)(x + 6) = 0$, its solutions are $x = 7$ and $x = -6$, so easy!

Frances did not agree. She pointed out: "Not every equation can be solved by factoring; therefore I like the method of quadratic formula. The method of formula is universal. Whether the answers are integers, fractions, irrational numbers, or even complex numbers, the formula is always applicable. For a quadratic equation $ax^2 + bx + c = 0$, we can always try to solve it by the quadratic formula $x = \dfrac{-b \pm \sqrt{b^2 - 4ac}}{2a}$. Oh, I understand that the calculation may be longer compared to the method of factoring, but many equations simply cannot be factored. For example the solutions of the equation $x^2 - 3x - 7 = 0$ are $x = \dfrac{3 + \sqrt{37}}{2}$ and $x = \dfrac{3 - \sqrt{37}}{2}$. Factoring method is useless in such a case. We need to rely on the method of quadratic formula."

"Good!" said Dr.C. "Since we are talking about the quadratic formula, let us consider one more question. Who can tell us, in the equation

$ax^2 + bx + c = 0$, what are the meanings of the three coefficients a, b, and c? What function does each coefficient have?"

Frances answered first: "I know the coefficient a. If $a > 0$ the curve opens up and has a minimum; if $a < 0$ the curve opens down and has a maximum. If $|a|$ is large, the curve becomes narrow. However I do not really know the meanings of the coefficients b and c."

Tom said: "c is the y-intercept, that is, the intersection of the parabola and the y-axis. In the expression $y = ax^2 + bx + c$, if $x = 0$ we have $y = c$. I also have to say that I don't know what the coefficient b means."

Dr.C told the students: "The coefficient b has its own meaning. Assume that a quadratic equation has two roots -5 and 3, if we only change b to $-b$, the two roots will switch signs, become 5 and -3. Here is an example, the equation $x^2 - 2x - 3 = 0$ has two roots -1 and 3 with the axis of symmetry $x = 1$. When we change the coefficient b to $-b$, the equation becomes $x^2 + 2x - 3 = 0$, with two roots 1 and -3. The axis of symmetry now is $x = -1$. When b is changed to $-b$ the parabola is reflected about the y-axis. The symmetric axis of the parabola is $x = -\dfrac{b}{2a}$. The x coordinate of the vertex is $-\dfrac{b}{2a}$, and the roots of the equation are $\dfrac{-b + \sqrt{b^2 - 4ac}}{2a}$ and $\dfrac{-b - \sqrt{b^2 - 4ac}}{2a}$ (if they exist)."

Dr.C then asked the students: "Is there anyone who likes the method of completing the squares?"

Wendy said: "I do. I like the method of completing the squares. Although it looks lengthy, it can give us the graph of the parabola directly. This method works for every quadratic equation, whether the roots are rational or irrational numbers. The vertex of the parabola $y = a(x - h)^2 + k$ is at (h, k) --- more than that, do not forget that the quadratic formula itself was derived from the method of completing the squares!"

Kelvin added: "When we try to find the optimal values (the maximum and the minimum) of a parabola, the method of completing the squares is effective. For example if we want to find two numbers such that their sum is 16, and the sum of their squares S is a minimum, then

$$S = x^2 + (16 - x)^2 = 2(x^2 - 16x + 128)$$

"Let us re-write this expression as $S = 2(x - 8)^2 + 128$ by the method of completing the squares. The vertex is $(8, 128)$. The minimum of the sum of the squares is 128, which occurs when $x = 8$ (and the other number $16 - x$ is also 8). Please note that, this equation has $b^2 - 4ac < 0$, so it does not have real roots."

Frances pointed out: "Wow, even when we do not have real roots, we can still find the vertex from the two complex roots. Your equation (by formula) has two roots $8 \pm 8i$ where $i = \sqrt{-1}$. Add the two roots $(8 + 8i) + (8 - 8i) = 16$ then divide the answer by 2, we get 8. So the x coordinate of the vertex is 8. Although in the process the roots went beyond real numbers, the answers fall back to real numbers."

Finally Dr.C suggested the class to give an overall summary about the three methods to solve a quadratic equation. Judy said: "Now we see that every method has its own advantage. The easy method is factoring but it only works if the roots are whole numbers or simple fractions. Many equations cannot be solved by factoring. However every quadratic equation can be solved by quadratic formula or by completing the squares. If you want to sketch the graph of a parabola, completing the squares would be your first choice. If all three methods are applicable, the method of factoring is the fastest. If you cannot factor an expression, don't worry, try quadratic formula or completing the squares, they work in all cases."

9.2 The fence law

Today Dr.C invited his friend Mr. Martin to sit in the mathematics classroom. You probably remember Mr. Martin (Chapter 2, section "The most cost-effective fence"). He is a successful farmer; one thing he does is building fences around his field. Last time Dr.C asked Mr. Martin and the students a question, "Can we use 1 more meter of fence to enclose 10000 m^2 additional area of a rectangular field?"

Today's lesson was given to high school students. Mr. Martin was excited and enthusiastic. He arrived at the class early. In the class Dr.C first asked the students an easy question: "If the perimeter of a rectangle is fixed, under what shape does the rectangle have the highest value of area? If the area of a rectangle is fixed, under what shape does it have the smallest value of perimeter?" The students immediately answered: "a square in both cases!"

"Good, you know those already," smiled Dr.C. "Now let us go further. If Mr. Martin wants to use 600 m fence to enclose the following shape field (see the diagram below), what should be the optimal length and width in order to enclose the maximum area?"

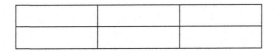

Such a question could not stop the high school students. Some of them used knowledge of quadratic functions; some of them used knowledge of calculus. The answers were: $x = 100$ m and $y = 75$ m. The total area enclosed in such a situation was $100 \times 75 = 7500$ m^2.

"Excellent," said Dr.C. "However, today I want to tell you, there is a quicker way. Such a question does not need any knowledge of quadratic functions or calculus; the conclusion can be obtained at a glance *before* you do any calculation. Believe it or not, I am going to tell you a law of my own. I call it 'the fence law'. You cannot find it from your textbooks. Let me tell you the 'fence law'."

"We may understand it this way: **'the Nature (or the God) is fair'. Exactly half of the fence must be used in one direction (say the north---south direction) and the other half in the perpendicular direction (the east---west direction).** The total length of Mr. Martin's fence is 600 m, therefore 300 m should be used in one direction and the other 300 m in the perpendicular direction. In the x direction there are three horizontal line segments so that each of them is 100 m long, and in the y direction there are four line segments so that each of them should be $300 \div 4 = 75$ m. Oh! The Nature is fair! You don't need high school math to know the answers!"

"Wow! it's so simple!" Cheered Mr. Martin and the students.

Dr.C continued: "Let us study the question in more depth. If the total length of the fence is not divided evenly in the north-south direction and the east-west direction, say if $x = 180$ m and $y = 15$ m, the total length of fence is still 600 m ($180 \times 3 + 15 \times 4 = 600$). However the area enclosed will only be $180 \times 15 = 2700$ m^2 instead of the 7500 m^2 obtained by 100×75. In average 1 m fence corresponds to an area 12.5 m^2 in the optimal case, but only 4.5 m^2 in that $180m \times 15m$ case. The efficiency is higher if we use the optimum way (the total x equals the total y).

"Using a certain length of fence to enclose an area as large as possible, that is equivalent to say using the shortest length of fence to enclose a fixed area lot. In both cases the answer is fair: the north - south direction total length is the same as the east - west direction total length.

"Let us do an exercise: If we use 1200 m fence to enclose a lot as shown in the following diagram, what should be its length and width such that the total enclosed area is the maximum?"

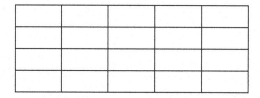

This time even Mr. Martin, who did not have enough knowledge of quadratic function or calculus, said immediately: "120 m in one way, 100 m in the other way!" Because there are 5 horizontal lines and 6 vertical lines. Half of 1200 is 600, $600 \div 5 = 120$ and $600 \div 6 = 100$, so easy!

Dr.C said: "Of course you can still use higher mathematics to find the answer by calculus or quadratic function. Nevertheless knowing the answer *before* you start any calculation is no doubt a wonderful thing. Even if one side is along a river or the grid is not divided evenly, still half horizontal and half vertical, our 'fence law' still works!

"There is a case such that we must apply the rule with caution --- when the x-dimension and the y-dimension are not equal in nature. For instance if the cost to build 1 m fence in the x-direction is different from the cost to build 1 m fence in the y-direction, then the total length of the fence is not evenly distributed in the two directions. However, the total cost in such a problem is still divided into two equal halves, one spent in the x-direction and the other spent in the y-direction. Think about it, this fence law is fair, it represents the most reasonable way."

Dr.C introduced the "fence law". Mr. Martin was very happy; he brought peanuts and fruits from his farm and invited the students to taste. A special mathematics class ended in cheers.

9.3   Complex roots of quadratic equations

When $b^2 - 4ac < 0$, the quadratic equation $ax^2 + bx + c = 0$ does not have real roots, only has complex roots.

Today Dr.C said: "The complex roots of a quadratic equation must be conjugate, tied to each other closely. The solutions of equation $x^2 - 6x + 13 = 0$ are $3 + 2i$ and $3 - 2i$. They cannot be unrelated (like $3 + 2i$ and $2 - 5i$). However, the real number roots of a quadratic equation seem to be unrelated (the roots of $x^2 + 5x - 6 = 0$ are 1 and -6). Can you explain that?"

Nancy said: "When we solve an equation $ax^2 + bx + c = 0$, the quadratic formula tells us that

$$x = \frac{-b \pm \sqrt{b^2 - 4ac}}{2a} = \frac{-b}{2a} \pm \frac{\sqrt{b^2 - 4ac}}{2a}.$$

"If $b^2 - 4ac < 0$, we get two roots in the format of $a \pm bi$, therefore the two complex roots must be conjugate."

Connie said: "Oh, I realize that actually the two *real* roots of a quadratic equation are **also related to each other by the same pattern**. For example, the equation $x^2 + 5x - 6 = 0$ has two roots 1 and −6. These two roots seem to be unrelated, but actually they are related in the same way $a \pm b$. The quadratic formula gives us the two solutions $-\frac{5}{2} \pm \frac{7}{2}$. What happened is that these two solutions appear unrelated when they are written as 1 and −6. If we solve the equation $6x^2 - 7x - 20 = 0$, we get two answers $\frac{5}{2}$ and $-\frac{4}{3}$, they look so different and unrelated, but actually they are related to each other tightly. The formula of quadratic equation actually produces these two solutions as $\frac{7}{12} + \frac{23}{12}$ and $\frac{7}{12} - \frac{23}{12}$."

People realized that apparently un-related things were actually closely related, still $a \pm b$.

Felix said: "We not only need to know that the two complex roots are conjugate, but also need to know *why* they are always conjugate, why they *cannot be unrelated*. The answer lies in the fact that the three coefficients of a quadratic equation are real numbers. Assume that the two roots are x_1 and x_2, the equation can be written as $(x - x_1)(x - x_2) = 0$. Let us first *assume* that the two roots are un-related, that is, they are $a + bi$ and $c + di$, then

$$[x - (a + bi)][x - (c + di)] = 0$$

expand:

$$x^2 + [(-a - c) + (-b - d)i]x + [(ac - bd) + (ad + bc)i] = 0.$$

152

"To guarantee that the coefficients (the two square brackets) are real numbers, we must have

$$\begin{cases} (-b-d) = 0 \\ (ad+bc) = 0 \end{cases}$$

"The first equation tells us that $d = -b$. Taking that into consideration, the second one tells us that $c = a$. Therefore $c + di$ is nothing but $a - bi$. Note that we first assume that the two solutions are $a + bi$ and $c + di$ unrelated, then we proved that, in order to guarantee that the coefficients of the equation are real numbers, the root $c + di$ actually is $a - bi$. So, the two solutions must be conjugate, $a + bi$ and $a - bi$."

The class applauded. Students praised Felix, Nancy and Connie for their thorough explanations. Dr.C continued on the topic and talked about the usefulness of complex numbers (see the next section).

9.4   Powerful complex numbers

Dr.C continued to talk about complex numbers. He said: "In our daily life, it seems to be that we don't need complex numbers and we don't use them. Everyday we use rational and irrational numbers like 0, -4, $\dfrac{2}{7}$, $\sqrt{3}$, etc. Who has ever seen a complex number in our daily life (like the age, weight, distance, money, student mark, time, speed, etc.)?

"However, complex numbers are useful. In mathematics without them the solutions of quadratic equations are not complete, equations like

$x^2 = -4$ or $2x^2 - 3x + 9 = 0$ would not have a solution. In higher mathematics there is a special branch called 'complex variable functions' to deal with functions with complex arguments. Complex numbers and complex variable functions are useful in physics and engineering too. At high school level we understand that complex numbers have two special properties, due to these two special properties they are unique in calculations.

"First, the value of i^n ($i = \sqrt{-1}$) follows a very strong pattern when n changes. The values of i, i^2, i^3, i^4 are $i, -1, -i$ and 1 respectively. If we continue, we will see that i^5, i^6, i^7, i^8 repeat the same pattern (equal to $i, -1, -i, 1$) and so on. Because of this pattern, to calculate $i = \sqrt{-1}$ to the power of any higher number is not a problem. To find what is i^{17295}, simply calculate $17295 \div 4$, ignore the quotient, and only look at the remainder. The remainder of this question is 3, according to the above pattern we know, $i^{17295} = -i$ (not hard).

"Secondly, complex numbers follow the de Moivre law. This law behaves similar to logarithms. It reduces the calculation by one level. In mathematics addition and subtraction make the lowest level of calculation; multiplication and division form the second level. The third level contains powers and roots like x^4 and $\sqrt[3]{x}$. The fourth level contains exponents and logarithms like 3^x and $\log_3 x$. When we deal with mixed levels we follow the rule that 'doing the higher level operation before doing the lower level operation'. The great power of logarithm is that it reduces the calculation by one level so that the process is simplified ($\log(mn) = \log m + \log n$, $\log m^n = n \log m$), multiplication becomes addition and exponent becomes multiplication. The de Moivre law of complex numbers does a similar thing: The n-th power of a complex number $a + bi = re^{i\theta}$ is $(re^{i\theta})^n = r^n e^{in\theta}$. Note that the angle only multiplies n, not to the nth power. The nth root of a complex number $z = r(\cos\theta + i\sin\theta)$ has n answers. For example $\sqrt[3]{z}$ has a module of $\sqrt[3]{r}$ and an angle of either $\dfrac{\theta}{3}$ or $\dfrac{\theta + 2\pi}{3}$ or $\dfrac{\theta + 4\pi}{3}$. In total there are 3 solutions. Why don't we continue to use $\dfrac{\theta + 6\pi}{3}$ or more?

Because $\dfrac{\theta + 6\pi}{3}$ is the same as $\dfrac{\theta}{3} + 2\pi$, which is the same as the angle $\dfrac{\theta}{3}$. Instead of the nth root, we divide the angle by n. The calculation goes down one level, and becomes easier. This is an example of *'converting hard to easy'*."

"Wow!" exclaimed the students: "Before today's class we thought that complex numbers make the calculation harder, now we realize that complex numbers make the evaluation easier. Using them the calculation can be reduced by one level and become easier. Complex numbers are useful, we will study the topic thoroughly, prepare for future university courses."

Chapter 10
Trigonometric Functions

10.1 The signs (+ or –) of trigonometric functions

How do we know whether a trigonometric function (example: $\sin\theta$, $\cos\theta$, or $\tan\theta$) of an angle is positive or negative? A way widely used in North America is to remember the "CAST rules". The word *CAST* helps us to remember the signs in the following way: In the diagram below, *C* means the region where $\cos\theta$ is positive, *S* means the region where $\sin\theta$ is positive, *T* means the region where $\tan\theta$ is positive, and *A* means the region where all trig functions are positive (the 1st quadrant).

$$
\begin{array}{c|c}
S & A \\
\hline
T & C
\end{array}
$$

Today Dr.C told the class: "We can develop a method better than the *CAST* rule.   Our method is called 'the *Circular Graph* method'. Using our circles not only can we decide the signs of a trig function, but also can find complete answers of a trig equation.

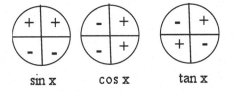

157

"Let us use the circles to help us solve an equation $\sin\theta = 0.5$ where $0° \le \theta \le 360°$. From the knowledge of special angles (or using a calculator) we can easily find the first solution $\theta = 30°$. Look at the circle of $\sin x$, the diagram clearly shows that $\sin x$ is positive in the first quadrant *and* the second quadrant. Therefore there should be another solution in the second quadrant. *By symmetry* it is $\theta = 150°$.

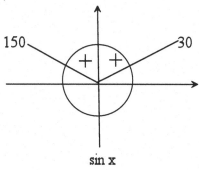

sin x

"Next, let us solve $\cos\theta = -\dfrac{2}{9}$ where $0° \le \theta \le 360°$. The first answer $103°$ can be found with a calculator. The circle of $\cos\theta$ tells us that in the third quadrant there exists another solution, which *by symmetry* is $257°$

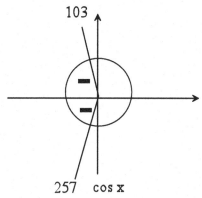

257   cos x

"As to the equation of $\tan\theta = -0.4$ where $0° \le \theta \le 360°$, the first answer $\theta = -22°$ can be found with a calculator. However, $0° \le \theta \le 360°$

requires the angle to be positive so we re-write the angle $-22°$ as $338°$, and then check the circle of $\tan\theta$. The circle tells us that in the second and the fourth quadrants the function $\tan\theta$ is negative. By symmetry $338° - 180° = 158°$ is the second answer. The two positions and the origin form a straight line.

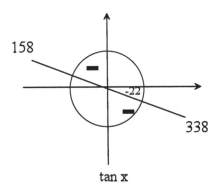

tan x

"Want to know the difference? By using our circular graph method we not only know whether a function is positive or negative, but can also find the second solution of a trig equation by symmetry. For $\sin\theta$ the two answers are symmetric to the y-axis. For $\cos\theta$ the two answers are symmetric to the x-axis. For $\tan\theta$ the two angles make a straight line through the origin. Our circular graph method makes the job of solving trigonometric equations easy."

10.2 Ambiguous cases of the sine law

When we apply the sine law to find the length of a side of a triangle, the answer is unique. On the other hand if we apply the sine law to solve an angle of a triangle we may face the possibility that for one value of $\sin\theta$ there exist two angles --- the second angle $(180° - \theta)$ is hidden. We must remind ourselves the possibility of the existence of the second angle.

Today Dr.C said: "Under what condition should we consider the existence of the second solution? A simple way of course is *just to assume* that there are two answers. Find $(180° - \theta)$ anyway. If it makes the sum of the three angles more than $180°$ discard it; otherwise accept it.

"However, even if the sum of internal angles equals $180°$, we may still have problems. Such problems could be even more difficult to recognize."

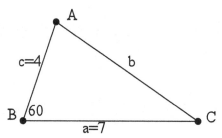

Dr.C drew a triangle on the white board: "Given that in $\triangle ABC$ two sides are $c = 4$ and $a = 7$, one internal angle $\angle B = 60°$, solve that triangle" Dr.C said. "Step one, apply the cosine law to find $b = \sqrt{37} = 6.0828$. If we only change $c = 4$ to $c = 3$ without any other change, b would still be the same, i.e. $b = \sqrt{37} = 6.0828$. Do you believe it?"

"That is amazing!" Students seemed not to believe it. However, a simple calculation proved that for both $c = 4$ and $c = 3$, the law of cosine led to the same conclusion: $b^2 = 4^2 + 7^2 - 2(4)(7)\cos 60° = 37$ and $b^2 = 3^2 + 7^2 - 2(3)(7)\cos 60° = 37$.

Next, they returned to the original question $c = 4$. To find the angle apply the sine law

$$\frac{\sin A}{7} = \frac{\sin 60^\circ}{6.0828}$$

From here we get $\sin A = 0.9966$ and $\angle A = 85^\circ$. So the third angle is $\angle C = 180^\circ - 60^\circ - 85^\circ = 35^\circ$.

Dr.C said: "Now, if we consider the possibility of ambiguous cases of the sine law, the second possible answer of $\angle A$ would be $\angle A = 180^\circ - 85^\circ = 95^\circ$, with $\angle C = 25^\circ$ and $\angle B = 60^\circ$. These three angles still satisfy that the sum of internal angles is 180° and that the larger angle faces the longer side. Sounds OK? Be careful! The second answer does not exist! When two sides and the angle between the two sides are given, the whole triangle (size and the shape) is fixed. It is easy to construct that triangle from the given information. Only one triangle can be made.

"If we did not solve the angle $\angle A$ first, instead we calculated the smaller angle $\angle C$ by the sine law, then we would have $\frac{\sin 60^\circ}{6.0828} = \frac{\sin C}{4}$ and $\angle C = 35^\circ$. Now if we still worry about ambiguity, the second possible answer of $\angle C$ is $180^\circ - 35^\circ = 145^\circ$ and that is impossible (since $145^\circ + 60^\circ > 180^\circ$). Thus, this question only has one set of solution (35°, 60° and 85°). Theoretically only when $b \sin A < a < b$ we have ambiguity. In this question $b \sin A < a$ but $a > b$, so there is no second answer."

"Here is another question", said Dr.C, "in the diagram below $a = 3$, $b = 14$ and $\angle B = 60^\circ$. Please solve $\triangle ABC$. Should there be two sets of answers or just one set?"

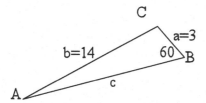

Unlike the previous question, this one did not give you two sides and the angle between them. Barbara found the side c by the law of cosine

$$14^2 = c^2 + 3^2 - 2(3)(c)\cos 60°$$

That was a quadratic equation $c^2 - 3c - 187 = 0$ with the solution $c = 15.3$ (discard the negative one). She applied the sine law:

$$\frac{\sin 60°}{14} = \frac{\sin C}{15.3}$$

And found $\angle C = 71°$, thus $\angle A = 49°$.

Destiny applied the sine law first.

$$\frac{\sin 60°}{14} = \frac{\sin A}{3}$$

She got $\angle A = 11°$. There was no ambiguous case because if there was, that second angle would be $180° - 11° = 169°$. That together with the given angle $60°$ would exceed $180°$. The question only had one set of solution $\angle C = 109°$ and $\angle A = 11°$.

162

Who was right? Destiny was right. This question only had one solution. The side length $a = 3$ was much smaller than $b = 14$, led to the conclusion that the angle $\angle A$ should be *much smaller* than $\angle B = 60°$. The answer $\angle A = 11°$ was more appropriate than $49°$.

As a summary, Dr.C said seriously: "My friends, please don't look down upon this question! The mistake that the first answer had was not obvious at a glance. If we were not careful, we might not be able to find the mistake. Note that the *first answer* was wrong. If we were satisfied and stopped there we got a wrong answer. If we were not satisfied and continued to find the second answer, ($\angle C = 180° - 71° = 109°$, $\angle A = 180° - \angle B - \angle C = 11°$) and presented both, we were *still wrong*. That question does not have two sets of answers, only one --- the *second* one, the *hidden* one. The correct answer is hidden, not the one we got first. By constructing the graph we see that there is only one solution."

Dr.C smiled, concluded the lesson.

10.3 Does the law of cosine have ambiguous cases?

It is well known that the sine law may have ambiguous cases. Can the cosine law also have a similar ambiguous situation? Dr.C said: "It is not written in textbooks, but the common point is clear: *no*. Why not? Because, if one angle of a triangle satisfies $\sin A = 0.5$, the answer could be either $\angle A = 30°$ or $150°$. For a triangle the second answer may be still acceptable. However if $\cos A = 0.5$ then $\angle A = 60°$ or $300°$. The second answer is not acceptable --- it is way too large."

However, Dr.C also pointed out: "If we apply the cosine law to find the *length* of a side of a triangle (not an angle), then there may come ambiguous cases. This is because that the nature of the cosine law is quadratic. A quadratic equation in many cases has two different roots. If both roots are acceptable (e.g., no negative answer, no result too large or too small), then we accept both answers.

"Example: Given that $c = 5$, $b = 4$, and $\angle B = 50°$, find the third side a of this triangle.

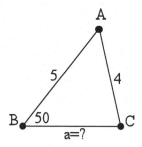

"According to the cosine law, $4^2 = 5^2 + a^2 - 2(5)a \cos 50°$. Such an equation is quadratic. It has two solutions $a = 4.4$ and $a = 2.1$, as shown in the diagram below. If we apply the sine law we get two sets of solutions. From this point of view, I would say that the law of cosine may also have ambiguous cases."

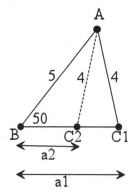

10.4 Can we have two cosine laws?

In all textbooks only one cosine law is introduced. In triangle $\triangle ABC$ we have $c^2 = a^2 + b^2 - 2ab\cos C$. Of course we may re-write the law as $a^2 = b^2 + c^2 - 2bc\cos A$ and $b^2 = a^2 + c^2 - 2ac\cos B$, but these are not considered as different laws, just the same law applied to different angles. All three expressions have the same nature.

However, today Dr.C told his students: "From my point of view we could have two *different* cosine laws. In the following diagram you see a parallelogram with two sides a and b, and an internal angle $\angle C$. The lengths of the two diagonals are c_1 and c_2:

$$c_1^2 = a^2 + b^2 - 2ab\cos C$$
$$c_2^2 = a^2 + b^2 + 2ab\cos C$$

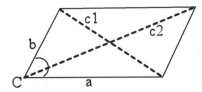

"The first one is the usual meaning cosine law. The second one changes one sign, − becomes +. **It is a new law**, different from the usual cosine law in nature. I call it 'the second cosine law'."

Dr.C said: "This 'second cosine law' has many applications. When we add two vectors like two forces or two velocities, such a law is useful. For example, a force of 100 N is added to a force of 80 N and the angle between them is $60°$, the situation is shown in the diagram below:

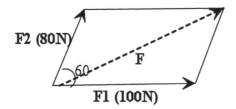

F2 (80N)

60°

F

F1 (100N)

"In vector notation the resultant force $\vec{F} = \vec{F_1} + \vec{F_2}$, the magnitude of the resultant force can be found by the *second* cosine law:

$$F^2 = 100^2 + 80^2 + 2(100)(80)\cos 60°$$

"Hence the resultant force is $F = 156$ N. Note that we use the addition sign here, not the subtraction sign as in usual cosine law. If we still want to apply the usual form cosine law we must use $180° - 60° = 120°$ angle instead of the given angle $60°$. Now you see, isn't the second cosine law also useful? I love it. The direction of the resultant force can be further obtained by applying the law of sine."

10.5 A comparison of $\sin\theta$, $\cos\theta$ and $\tan\theta$

It was getting cooler day by day. The fall season arrived. Dr.C thought it would be useful and interesting to compare the three primary trigonometric functions $\sin\theta$, $\cos\theta$ and $\tan\theta$, now that the students had already learned all of them.

Today Dr.C discussed that with the class. "Relax, there is no restriction. You are encouraged to say anything about the three trig functions," said Dr.C enthusiastically.

Maya said first: "I think all trigonometric functions are beautiful. Among them I like $\sin\theta$ most. It is so nice, the curve of $\sin\theta$ is soft, smooth and beautiful. In my eyes the curve of a sine function is a beauty. Her curve undulates gently, without sudden up or down and never rushes to infinity. Such a smooth and pretty curve brings joy to people who are learning trigonometry. Certainly, the curve of cosine is as beautiful as the curve of sine. They are twin sisters, very similar but still distinguishable. A smooth slide of one produces the other."

Owen said: "I like the tangent function. Like a warrior, the curve of a tangent function links the horizontal horizon (mother Earth, the ground) with the vertical line (buildings, cliffs). It is the most useful function with many practical applications. As the angle approaches $90°$, the value of tangent approaches infinity. Starting from the same point 0, a sine function reaches 1 at $\theta = 90°$, whereas a tangent function reaches the same height only at $45°$, much faster. From there it rushes to infinity without hesitation. It increases its value more and more rapidly --- so brave, unstoppable and unbreakable. At close to $\theta = 90°$, its function value increases a lot with every 0.1 degree increase of the angle. What a hero it is!"

"Moreover," said Anthony. "The period of a sine function or a cosine function is $360°$, yet the period of a tangent function is only $180°$. Tangent function circulates faster."

Carmela said: "When these three primary trig functions meet together, they behave like three siblings of one family. Brothers, sisters are related to each other and tied closely, $\tan\theta = \dfrac{\sin\theta}{\cos\theta}$. You can find anyone from the other two members of the trig function family."

Sophia raised a question: "We know that the maximum value of $\sin\theta$ and $\cos\theta$ is 1, while there is no limit of a tangent function. A tangent function reaches 1 at $\theta = 45°$ and after that it is always greater than 1. Bases on these, can we say that for the same angle we always have $\tan\theta > \sin\theta$?"

After some debate Michelle said: "Not always. In the first quadrant it is true; the value of tangent is always greater than the value of sine function for the same angle. Such a conclusion is also correct in the third quadrant where the function $\sin\theta$ is negative and the function $\tan\theta$ is positive --- so that $\tan\theta > \sin\theta$. If the angle is $0°$, $180°$, or $360°$ etc., the two functions have the same value 0."

Jeffrey pointed out: "Nevertheless, when the angle is in the second quadrant, $\sin\theta$ is positive and $\tan\theta$ is negative, the conclusion must be $\sin\theta > \tan\theta$ there."

"How is the situation when the angle is in the fourth quadrant?" Tania asked.

"Well," answered Helen: "When the angle is in the fourth quadrant, both $\sin\theta$ and $\tan\theta$ are negative. The conclusion is $\sin\theta > \tan\theta$. Why? In the diagram below $\sin\theta = \dfrac{a}{c}$ and $\tan\theta = \dfrac{a}{b}$. Note that a is negative, b and the hypotenuse c are positive and $c > b$. Therefore we have $0 > \sin\theta > \tan\theta$. (Example: $a = -3$, $b = 4$ and $c = 5$, as shown in the diagram, then $0 > -\dfrac{3}{5} > -\dfrac{3}{4}$.) Another example could be that $\sin 320° = -0.643$ whereas $\tan 320° = -0.839$."

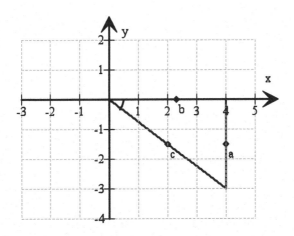

Tania said: "I see. There are two regions where $\tan\theta$ is greater, the 1st quadrant and the 3rd quadrant. There are also two regions where $\sin\theta$ is greater (the 2nd quadrant and the 4th quadrant). When the angle is $0°$, $180°$, or $360°$ etc., they equal to each other. Finally, if the angle is $90°$ or $270°$, $\tan\theta$ does not exist at all, there the comparison does not have a meaning."

Students applauded.

What a vivid math lesson! Dr.C was very happy. He added a final remark at the end of the lesson: "We know that, for a first quadrant angle its sine function increases slower than the tangent function of the same angle. However, to draw a conclusion that we do not need to be accurate enough when we calculate the value of a sine function is improper. Even a sine or cosine function could change fast. For instance if $\cos\theta = 0.994$, then $\theta = 6.28°$. If we round the given number to $\cos\theta = 0.99$, then we have $\theta = 8.11°$. The error is 29%. The relative error is quite large, isn't it?"

10.6 Mysterious trigonometric identities

Today's class was special. Dr.C did not teach trigonometry directly, instead, he challenged the students by saying: "Everybody, we know that multiplication is not addition, the product of two numbers in general is different from the sum of the same two numbers. However, can you still find two numbers (except 0 and 0) such that their sum is the same as their product?"

"That's not hard!" Students answered immediately. "2 and 2. The sum of 2 and 2 is 4, the product of 2 and 2 is still 4."

"Good," said Dr.C, "but can you find another example?"

The class became silent. To find another example seemed not so easy.

(In many cases the sum is less than the product (like 3 and 2, or 10 and 9); in some other cases the sum is greater than the product (like 1 and 0, or 0.1 and 10). Is there any pair --- other than 2 and 2, 0 and 0 ---that the sum equals the product?)

David got his answer: $\dfrac{5}{2}$ and $\dfrac{5}{3}$

$$\frac{5}{2} + \frac{5}{3} = \frac{15}{6} + \frac{10}{6} = \frac{25}{6}$$

$$\frac{5}{2} \times \frac{5}{3} = \frac{25}{6}$$

"Right," said Dr.C. "Let us come back to trigonometry. In trigonometry there are several identities quite special. Let us study $\sec^2 \theta + \csc^2 \theta = \sec^2 \theta \times \csc^2 \theta$ first. It can be proved that this is an identity correct for *any* angle θ. Well, that is to say, for any angle θ, the sum and the product of the two parts are *always* the same. This identity is correct for all angles, how can that be true? The sum equals the product, not only for a specific angle, but for any angle!"

The class showed great interest. Dr.C continued: ``This question is not as hard as it looks. Let us consider the equation $b + a = ab$ (sum equals product). Divide both sides by ab, we get $\dfrac{1}{a} + \dfrac{1}{b} = 1$. Well, now we see that two numbers satisfy the requirement that their sum equals their product, must satisfy the equation $\dfrac{1}{a} + \dfrac{1}{b} = 1$ first. The sum of their reciprocals must be 1. David's answer $\dfrac{5}{2}$ and $\dfrac{5}{3}$ satisfy this requirement because $\dfrac{2}{5} + \dfrac{3}{5}$ is 1. As to $\sec^2 \theta$ and $\csc^2 \theta$, their reciprocals are $\cos^2 \theta$ and $\sin^2 \theta$. Since $\sin^2 \theta + \cos^2 \theta = 1$, the above property holds. To any angle in the common domain of $\sec \theta$ and $\csc \theta$ this identity always holds.

"Such an identity is for addition and multiplication. The difference of two numbers can also be the same as the product. Try to find the condition for that to be true, then you will understand why $\tan^2 \theta - \sin^2 \theta = \tan^2 \theta \sin^2 \theta$ and $\cot^2 \theta - \cos^2 \theta = \cot^2 \theta \cos^2 \theta$ are always correct. These two identities are correct for any angle θ in the common domain of the given functions. Try to find the conditions first. Girls and boys, go ahead, give it a try!"

171

10.7 One hexagon helps us remember twelve identities

There are so many relations among the six trigonometric functions. Students want to know, is there any method to remember all of them?

Dr.C says: "Yes, there is one way. When I was a high school student my math teacher taught us a hexagon. Such a hexagon easily showed 12 relations of the six trig functions. Just think: connecting 12 formulas by one hexagon! It was amazing. (My high school --- the Shishi High School in Chengdu, Sichuan Province, China --- was established in the year 141 B.C. We celebrated her 2100 years birthday when I was a student there)."

Here is the diagram of the hexagon:

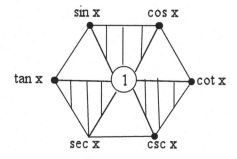

"On the right side of the diagram the function is the 'co-function' of the one on the left side (for example, $\cos x$ is the co-function of $\sin x$). This diagram contains 12 formulas in it. There are three ways to read the hexagon.

"First, the *straight line rule*: the two ends of any straight line are reciprocals of each other. When you multiply the two functions linked by a straight line the answer is the 1 at the center. There are three pairs;

$(\sin x)(\csc x) = 1$, $(\cos x)(\sec x) = 1$, $(\tan x)(\cot x) = 1$. Indeed you may consider them as the definitions of $\csc x$, $\sec x$, and $\cot x$.

"Second, *around the hexagon rule.* If we start with $\tan x$, move around the hexagon clockwise, the next two functions are $\sin x$ and $\cos x$. Then we have a relation $(\tan x)(\cos x) = \sin x$ (which is the same as $\tan x = \dfrac{\sin x}{\cos x}$). Continue to move around the hexagon; whenever you go 3 steps, the middle one is equal to the product of the one before it and one after it. So we have six relations this way; $(\sin x)(\cot x) = \cos x$, $(\cos x)(\csc x) = \cot x$, $(\cot x)(\sec x) = \csc x$, $(\csc x)(\tan x) = \sec x$, $(\sec x)(\sin x) = \tan x$, $(\tan x)(\cos x) = \sin x$.

"Third, the *triangle rule.* Please see the three shaded triangles in the diagram. Each of them has two vertices lying flat on the top, and one vertex below. Similar to the Pythagorean Theorem we have $\sin^2 x + \cos^2 x = 1$, $\tan^2 x + 1 = \sec^2 x$, and $\cot^2 x + 1 = \csc^2 x$.

"See, by just remembering one hexagon, we remember so many relations (altogether twelve trigonometric identities)!"

10.8 Is there a tangent law?

Jack asks Dr.C: "We have learned the sine law and the cosine law. Is there a law of tangent?"

"Yes," answers Dr.C. "The expression of tangent law is

$$\frac{\tan\dfrac{A+B}{2}}{\tan\dfrac{A-B}{2}} = \frac{a+b}{a-b}$$

"Why not check the theorem with an example? This way is to 'verify' the theorem, not to prove it. If a specific example holds, we cannot guarantee it is a truth. However if any one example fails, the theorem does not stand. We know that there is a special triangle with internal angles $90°$, $30°$, $60°$. If the shortest side length is 1, then the other two sides are $\sqrt{3}$ and 2 respectively. The left side of the tangent law now is $\dfrac{\tan\frac{90°+30°}{2}}{\tan\frac{90°-30°}{2}} = \dfrac{\tan 60°}{\tan 30°} = \dfrac{\sqrt{3}}{\frac{1}{\sqrt{3}}} = 3$, and the right side is $\dfrac{2+1}{2-1} = 3$. So the tangent law holds in this case.

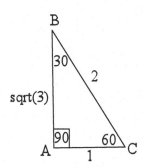

"Even if the triangle is not a right triangle the law of tangent is still correct. The following triangle has side length $a = 10$, angle $\angle A = 80°$ and angle $\angle B = 60°$. Apply the sine law $\dfrac{\sin 80°}{10} = \dfrac{\sin 60°}{b}$ we can find that $b = 8.7938524$. Now the tangent law becomes $\dfrac{\tan 70°}{\tan 10°} = \dfrac{18.7938524}{1.2061476}$, which is correct.

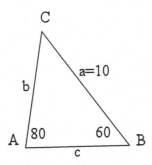

"Because the tangent law is complicated and is not as useful as the sine law and the cosine law, textbooks usually ignore them."

10.9 Two words help us study related, correlated angles

Some of Dr.C's students recently face a problem while studying trigonometry. There are too many formulas and relations of related angles and correlated angles. Of course, each relation could be derived one at a time from the basic laws. For instance, if we wanted to know $\cos(90° + \theta)$, we could derive the formula by

$$\cos(90° + \theta) = \cos 90° \cos \theta - \sin 90° \sin \theta$$
$$= 0(\cos \theta) - 1(\sin \theta) = -\sin \theta$$

Today, students asked Dr.C: "Isn't it boring to do every question this way?   Is there any short cut to help us write down formulas like $\cos(90° + \theta) = -\sin \theta$ directly and immediately?"

"Oh, yes!" said Dr.C. "The job is easy. You just need to remember two things:

1. quadrant   2. odd or even

"The first word (quadrant) is to check the quadrant of the angle. Note that we always treat θ as a small angle. Since θ is a small angle, $90° + \theta$ is in the second quadrant where the cosine function is negative. Therefore the first thing we know is that the answer of $\cos(90° + \theta)$ should have a negative sign in front.

"The second word (odd, or even) is to check the number. If you see an odd number multiple of $90°$, i.e., $90°$ multiplied by 1, 3, 5, 7 etc., then make a change. Sine changes to cosine, cosine changes to sine. (similarly for tangent and co-tangent, secant and co-secant). If you see an even multiple of $90°$, i.e., $180°$, $360°$, etc., then do not make such a change sine is still sine, cosine is still cosine, etc.

"In the above example $\cos(90° + \theta)$, the number is $90°$, so we should change cosine to sine. We already know that the sign is negative so $\cos(90° + \theta) = -\sin\theta$. Isn't that simple? "

Dr.C continued: "Although we always treat θ as a small angle, the formulas we obtained work for all θ values large or small. The order should not be reversed, we must consider quadrant (positive or negative sign) *before* we decide 'change or no change'. For our example $\cos(90° + \theta)$, if we reverse the order and consider 'change or no change' first, $(90° + \theta)$ would lead to a change (cosine becomes sine); and a sine function would produce a positive sign in the second quadrant (hence the final answer sign is wrong). If we decide the sign first, there would be no chance for such an error to

176

happen. At the first step we only see the given cosine function, and it is negative in the second quadrant. Remember to decide 'change or no change' at the second step, *after* we get a correct sign.

" Wow, this method is so powerful. **You will love it!** Let us prove the following trig identity:

$$\frac{\sin(\pi - x)\cot(\frac{\pi}{2} - x)\cos(2\pi - x)}{\tan(\frac{\pi}{2} + x)\tan(\pi + x)} = -\sin^2 x$$

"Using the two word method, each member of the left side can quickly be revised so that

$$LS = \frac{\sin x \tan x \cos x}{(-\cot x)\tan x} = \frac{\sin x \cos x}{(-\cot x)} = \frac{\sin x \cos x}{-\frac{\cos x}{\sin x}} = -\sin^2 x = RS$$

"The work is done! You are encouraged to use the original way, expand each part according to the expansion formulas of $\sin(A - B)$, $\cos(A - B)$, $\tan(A + B)$ and $\tan(A - B)$. The process would be very long and complicated. You will love the 'two word method', which makes the process simpler and easier."

Finally, Dr.C pointed out: "If you are to prove a trig identity, you know that the left side should equal to the right side. Therefore build a confidence before you start. Strongly believe that the original statement *can be* and *must be* proved, then work through it. If one way does not work, try a different approach. In many questions you may change $\tan x$, etc. into sine and cosine first to speed up the proving process. If you still find it hard, that may not be due to your lack of trig knowledge. Instead, the reason could be a weakness on other parts of math. For example, you may not know how to treat the composite fractions in the above example ($\dfrac{\sin x \cos x}{-\frac{\cos x}{\sin x}}$), or you may have a weakness in adding or subtracting rational expressions. Grasping algebra well will prepare you to handle trigonometry successfully."

10.10 Fast way to sketch trigonometric graphs

To sketch a trigonometric graph may be tedious lengthy work. Say, in order to sketch the curve of $y = 5\sin 2(\theta - \dfrac{\pi}{4}) - 1$ (the following diagram), first we sketch a curve $y = \sin\theta$ (shown as light solid curve), then multiply the amplitude of that curve by 5 (light dashed curve), reduce the period from 2π to π (light dotted curve), then slide this curve right $\dfrac{\pi}{4}$ (bold dashed curve), and finally move that curve down by 1 unit (bold solid curve). If there is a negative sign in front (5 becomes -5) we need one more curve. As a result five or six curves overlap each other, shown in one diagram making it hard to draw and difficult to read.

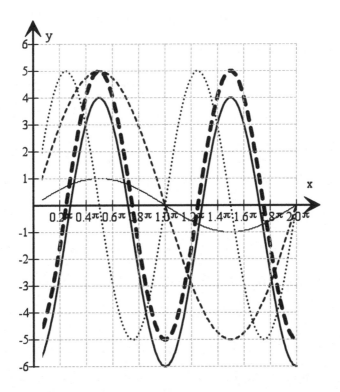

Students therefore ask Dr.C: "How can we sketch a trig curve faster and cleaner, without so many steps?"

Dr.C answers: "Making things simple is always our goal. Let me introduce a simpler way to sketch trig curves. Through **only two steps** we can sketch a complicated trig curve.

"Step1, consider the amplitude and the period only, forget the vertical and horizontal shifts. That is, for the curve $y = 5\sin 2(\theta - \frac{\pi}{4}) - 1$, we sketch $y = 5\sin 2\theta$ first. This is a normal sine curve with amplitude 5 and period π, shown as the solid curve in the diagram below. You could even draw a normal sine shape curve first without numbers, then write down

179

5 and −5 on the vertical axis indicating the maximum and minimum values, and write down π on the horizontal axis at the place of one period.

"Step 2, move the curve right by $\dfrac{\pi}{4}$ and down by 1, and the final curve is there (shown as the dotted curve). Please compare our simple two curve diagram with the above five curve mixed graph, which one is simpler? **Simple is beautiful**, does our two step method simplify the process of trigonometric curve sketching?"

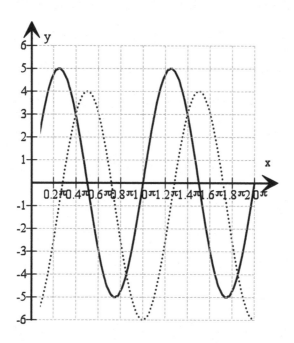

Chapter 11
Sequence and Series

11.1 Arithmetic and geometric sequence and series

A string of numbers is called a sequence if the numbers follow the same rule. Adding those numbers one by one we get a series. Sometimes the pattern may not be obvious. For example 5, 2, 3, 10, 37, 138...; they follow a recursive formula $t_n = 4t_{n-1} - t_{n-2}$ where $t_1 = 5$ and $t_2 = 2$.

The rule of an arithmetic series is simple: the difference between adjacent terms is a constant. The sum of the first n terms is $S_n = \dfrac{n}{2}(a + t_n)$. Dr.C points out; we better write this formula as $S_n = \left(\dfrac{a + t_n}{2}\right)n$. Why? Because $\left(\dfrac{a + t_n}{2}\right)$ is the mean value of the first term and the last term, hence is the average value of all the terms. Example: If the series is 1+5+9+13, the mean value is $\left(\dfrac{1+13}{2}\right) = 7$. This formula tells us that we can replace the series (1+5+9+13) by (7+7+7+7), some terms are increased and some are decreased but the sum does not change.

Textbooks often give another form of the first n terms of an arithmetic series $S_n = \dfrac{n}{2}(2a + (n-1)d)$. Dr.C points out; again it is better to write that formula in the form of $S_n = na + \dfrac{1}{2}n(n-1)d$. What is the difference? For any value of n (odd or even), the expression $\dfrac{1}{2}n(n-1)$ is always an integer, making the evaluation easier.

If every term of an arithmetic series is greater than its preceding one, can we say that the sum of the series is greater than the last term in the series ($S_n > t_n$)? One may agree with this statement. However that is not always correct. S_n indeed can be greater than the last term (as in 1+2+3), but S_n may also be equal to t_n (as in $-1+1+3$); and can be smaller than t_n too, (as in $(-2) + (-1) + 0$).

The sum of the first n terms of a geometric series is $S_n = \dfrac{a(1 - r^n)}{1 - r}$. If the common ratio between adjacent terms $r > 1$, the formula can be written as $S_n = \dfrac{a(r^n - 1)}{r - 1}$ to avoid negative numbers. When $-1 < r < 1$, the sum of infinite terms of a geometric series is $\lim_{n \to \infty} S_n = \dfrac{a}{1 - r}$. Dr.C says that we should pay attention to the n in these formulas. If you see a geometric series $1 + x + x^2 + x^3 + \cdots + x^n$, what is the expression of the total value? Note that here the n in the expression is not the n in the sum of series formula. Be aware that this series has $n+1$ terms, not n terms. The sum of all terms is actually S_{n+1}.

The difference between an arithmetic sequence and a geometric sequence is the difference between addition, subtraction and multiplication, division. If a sequence is arithmetic and geometric at the same time, it can only be a constant sequence (like 3, 3, 3).

There was a famous story about series and sequence. A minister who invented chess asked the emperor to award him in the following way: "Place one grain in the first cell of a chess board, place 2 in the second, 4 in the third and 8 in the fourth, etc". At first it looked easy for the emperor, but later the emperor found that the amount to be awarded became a huge astronomical figure. When $n = 64$, both t_n and S_n of this geometric series were far beyond the level that the emperor or his kingdom could afford. If we replace the geometric sequence in this story by an arithmetic sequence (1, 2, 3, 4 ...) then the sum of all 64 cells is merely 2080 grains. Dr.C laughs: "Needless to mention the emperor, even yours truly, me, can easily pay that minister, --- ha --- ha!"

11.2 Study triangles with the help of sequence

After talking about arithmetic and geometric sequence and series, Dr.C feels that he still has something more to say. He discusses the application of sequence and series in geometry.

"If the three internal angles of a triangle form an arithmetic sequence, can you find out how many degrees is one of the three internal angles?

"We only know that the three angles form an arithmetic sequence. That is not enough for us to figure out how large the greatest angle or the smallest angle is. But we are able to determine the middle angle, it is $60°$.

Why? Because $a + (a + d) + (a + 2d) = 180°$ where a is the smallest angle and d is the common difference. Thus we have $3a + 3d = 180°$ so that $a + d = 60°$. This is the size of the middle angle. The three angles could be $50°, 60°, 70°$; or could be (say) $43°, 60°, 77°$, or other combinations. The middle size angle however can only be $60°$ (If it is a right angle triangle the three angles are uniquely determined: $30°, 60°, 90°$).

"If the three sides of a right triangle form an arithmetic sequence, can we find the three internal angles?

"Again this is completely possible. In this problem we are not given any number or any information about what kind of arithmetic sequence it is. We don't know either a or d, how can we find specific degrees of all three angles? However the fact is, because it is a right angle triangle, the 'impossible' task becomes possible. This time let us call the middle side length as a, the Pythagorean theorem tells us that $(a - d)^2 + a^2 = (a + d)^2$. Expand it and we have $a = 4d$ so that the three sides are $3d$, $4d$ and $5d$. Apply the cosine law of trigonometry we can find the three angles one by one. The answers are $36.87°$, $53.13°$ and $90°$. Such three angles form a ratio relation 1: 1.44: 2.44 (not 3: 4: 5 as the sides). How large is the triangle? That is unable to determine since we only know the angles and the shape of the triangle, it could be a large area triangle or a smaller one.

"Why not assume the smallest side as a this time? It will still be correct but we will deal with quadratic equations instead of linear equation. So we better assume the middle side length as a.

"What happens if the three angles form a geometric sequence? Can we still find each angle? This time the answer is *no*. We can write the sum of the three angles as $a + ak + ak^2 = 180$. Such an equation has two

184

unknowns a and k, therefore it is impossible to uniquely decide the angles. A set of answers like (in degrees) 20, 47.45, 112.55; or 30, 53.74, 96.26 etc, is possible. If we add a condition that this triangle is a right triangle, then the largest angle is $90°$. The equation now becomes $90 + 90k + 90k^2 = 180$, i.e. $k^2 + k - 1 = 0$, with the solution $k = 0.618$. Hence the three angles are 34.38, 55.62, 90 (in degrees). The three sides form a different ratio $1:1.46:1.77$.

"If the three sides of a right triangle form a geometric sequence, can we find its three internal angles?

"Let us see, because it is a right triangle, the three sides satisfy the Pythagorean theorem. If we call the three sides a, ar and ar^2, then $(ar^2)^2 = (ar)^2 + a^2$. Cancel a^2 and we have $r^4 = r^2 + 1$. If we define k as r^2, we have an equation of k, $k^2 - k - 1 = 0$, with the solution $k = 1.618$, $r = \sqrt{k} = 1.272$. (Note that this ratio 1.618 is the reciprocal of the number 0.618 obtained from above). The three angles are (in degrees) 38.17, 51.83 and 90. The ratio of the three sides are $1:1.272:1.618$. Although the length of each side and the area of the triangle are not certain, its shape is known.

"If the triangle is not a right triangle, then even if we know its three sides form a geometric sequence, the triangle's shape is still unable to be uniquely decided."

11.3   Future value and present value

Belly and Shirley felt somewhat confused about the investment math they learned from the school: "There are too many formulas, too many situations.   Which formula should be applied to solve a certain type problem?"

Dr.C answered: "About your question, no problem, let us go step by step. Assume you deposit $3600 in a bank, how much money will you have three years from now? The answer of course depends on the interest rate of that bank. Let us start with the simplest case --- assume that there is no interest at all."

The students answered immediately: "Still $3600."

"Correct," said Dr.C. "If the interest rate is 6% annually without compounding, that is, the interest you earn will not be put back into your account to earn the 'interest of interest', then, how much money will you have after 3 years?"

Belly answered: "This is a simple interest question. Each year the interest will be $3600 \times 0.06 = 216$ dollars. In three years the total interest is 216×3 and the amount in the account is still $3600."

"Right," said Dr.C.   "If the interest is compound interest, which means the interest earned is put back into your account to earn interest, what will happen?"

Shirley said: "Oh, the value depends on the compound period. Assume that the annual rate is the same (6%) but compounded monthly, then in the three years time (36 months) we have $A = P(1+i)^n = 3600(1+0.005)^{36} = 4308.05$ dollars.   In this calculation

P is the principal (the initial deposit $3600), i is the interest rate per compound period (per month in this question), since the annual rate is 6%, the monthly rate is $i = \dfrac{0.06}{12} = 0.005$; n is the total number of compound periods, in this question the time is 3 years, therefore n is 36 months."

"Good," said Dr.C. "Now you have more money than in the simple interest case. You have $4308.05 in this compounded interest case, while in the simple interest case you only have $3600 plus the interest $216 \times 3 = \$648$. You get **$60.05** more. The more frequent the interest is compounded, the higher yield you will get. The scenario of this compound interest problem is similar to the situation that you deposit $3600 once into this account, and then sleep for three years. When you wake up three years later, you discover that your money increases to $4308.05.

"Let us go further, if you deposit $100 each month for 36 months, is the result same as if you deposit $3600 once at the beginning of the 3 years?"

After some thought Belly replied: "No, not the same. If you deposit regularly $100 each month it is a 'future value' problem. I am confused about the future value and the present value. Can you tell me the difference between them?"

"No problem," said Dr.C. "This time it is a 'deposit the same amount into an account again and again regularly, withdraw only once at the end of the period' problem. The final value (the *future value* FV) is

$$FV = R\left(\frac{(1+i)^n - 1}{i}\right)$$

"Assume the interest is the same as above (6% per year, compounded monthly) then $i = \dfrac{0.06}{12} = 0.005$, $n = 3 \times 12 = 36$, the value three years later will be

$$FV = 100 \left(\frac{(1+0.005)^{36} - 1}{0.005} \right) = \$3933.61\,"$$

Dr.C continued: "On the other hand, if you deposit only once then withdraw a fixed amount again and again regularly, until there is no money left, this time it is a *present value* (PV) question. Assume you deposit $3600 into the bank, withdraw a fixed amount every month for 36 months until no money is left, how much can you withdraw every month? The answer is more than $3600 \div 36 = 100$ dollars per month, because your money earns interest in this period. If the rate of interest is the same as above (6% annually compounded monthly), the calculation is:

$$PV = R \left(\frac{1 - (1+i)^{-n}}{i} \right)$$

$$3600 = R \left(\frac{1 - (1+0.005)^{-36}}{0.005} \right)$$

"The answer is R = $109.52. In the three years you get in total $109.52 \times 36 = 3942.72$ dollars. Compared to the initial deposit $3600, you actually get $342.72 more, that is the interest you have earned in the 3 years."

Finally, Dr.C told Shirley, Belly and other students a useful tip: "Under what situation should we apply the FV formula, and under what situation should we use the PV formula? I can tell you a tip. Just look at the (absolute) value of the balance, see **whether it should increase or decrease.**

188

When you deposit again and again the balance should increase, in that case we apply the FV formula. If you open an annuity, put in some money then withdraw the same amount again and again, the balance should become less and less, in that situation we apply the PV formula. If you borrow a loan from the bank and pay back regularly, the amount you owe the bank will decrease. If today you borrow $100000, next year you might only owe the bank $98000 or so. Do not view the amount of a loan as a negative number, only note its absolute value, then the value becomes less and less (from $100000 to $98000 in one year), when you see that decrease, you know it is a present value problem and apply the PV formula. Assume that you borrow $3600 from a bank, the interest is the same as above, then the calculation is exactly the same as above. Each month you should pay the bank $109.52. In three years you have given the bank $3942.72 to cover the $3600 borrowed at the beginning. As to the difference, $3942.72 - 3600 = \$342.72$, that is the interest you pay the bank.

"Therefore if the number increases use the FV formula, if the number decreases use the PV formula."

"Wow! so nice", said Belly and Shirley, "We like this tip. Can you please teach us something about mortgage?"

11.4 Secret of mortgage calculation

Dr.C continued: "It seems to be a mystery how banks calculate the mortgages. You go to a bank, apply for a mortgage, receive the answer and know how much you pay each month, but you do not know how the number was calculated. Let us talk about it today."

[A simple case]

"Helen wants to buy a house. The price after tax is $200000. Helen has $50000 prepared as the down payment. She needs to borrow $150000 from the bank and pay off the mortgage in 25 years. The interest rate is 8% annually compounded semi-annually. How much does Helen pay each month for the mortgage?

Step 1: Calculate the monthly interest rate.

Using the compound interest formula $A = P(1+i)^n$, we have $(1+i)^{12} = (1+0.04)^2$, where the 0.04 is the interest rate per compound period (1 year 8%, half a year 4%). In one year the interest is compounded twice so we have the right side. On the left side we have 12 months (a year). The solution of the monthly rate is $i = 0.0065582$. Note that we keep many decimals here to make the result accurate.

Step 2: Calculate the monthly payment using the present value (PV) formula

$$150000 = R\left(\frac{1-(1+0.0065582)^{-300}}{0.0065582}\right)$$

In this formula 300 is 25×12, number of months in 25 years. The answer is that each month Helen needs to pay the bank $R = \$1144.82$. Be accurate to one cent when you get the final answer. Helen actually pays the bank $1144.82 \times 300 = 343446$ dollars in 25 years, compare this to the amount she borrowed at the beginning ($150000), the difference $193446 is the interest. As you see, 56% of the money goes to the bank as interest."

[A more complicated case]

"Assume in the above example, the first mortgage is only set for 5 years, it renews at the end of the 5 year period with the new interest rate at that time. If the rate becomes 6% annually ever since that time, how much money can Helen save due to this drop of interest rate?

The key is that we must calculate *backwards* from the end of the 25 years. The total length of time is 25 years, after 5 years there will be 20 years (240 months) left. Question: At the end of the first 5 years how much does Helen owe the bank?

$$PV = 1144.82\left(\frac{1-(1+0.0065582)^{-240}}{0.0065582}\right) = 138203.58$$

It can be seen that in the first 5 years only a small portion of the borrowed money is paid, 92% of the borrowed amount $150000 you still owe.

Follow the way above $(1+i)^{12} = (1+\frac{0.06}{2})^2$, we convert 6% annually into 0.0049386 monthly, therefore

$$138203.58 = R\left(\frac{1-(1+0.0049386)^{-240}}{0.0049386}\right)$$

$R = \$984.27$

How much is saved? Each month Helen saves $1144.82 - 984.27 = 160.55$ dollars. In 20 years (240 months) she will save a total of $160.55 \times 240 = \$38532$ due to the decrease of the interest rate in the later 20 years."

After this discussion Belly, Shirley and other students understood the mortgage. Shirley said: "Wow, now I understand why all bank buildings are so tall and magnificent." Belly said: "In the future when I grow up and want to buy a house, I will do a calculation first. Today's talk prepares me for future financial planning. Thank you, Dr.C!"

11.5 Flow chart to study alternating series

Ophelia and friends are learning the convergence and divergence of series. An alternating series $a_0 - a_1 + a_2 - a_3 + \ldots$ can be written as $\sum (-1)^n a_n$ where $a_n > 0$. Ophelia does not understand alternating series. She asks Dr.C, is there a good method to determine whether an alternating series is converging or diverging?

Dr.C says: "Don't worry. Let me tell you three steps. Through these three steps you can decide the behavior of alternating series. Step 1, ignore the negative signs, and ask yourself whether the positive series $a_0 + a_1 + a_2 + a_3 + \ldots$ is converging or not. Since you ignore all negative signs now every term must be positive or zero, so the sum of the series must not be smaller than the original series. If the new series is converging, then the original alternating series must be converging (it is called 'absolute convergence' or AC). However if the new (all positive) series is diverging, then there is no conclusion about the original one. Make sure you understand this: if the bigger one goes to infinity, the smaller one may go to infinity too and may also be just finite. If the bigger one is limited, the smaller one cannot approach infinity, Isn't it reasonable?

"Next (step 2), ask yourself whether $\lim_{n \to \infty} a_n = 0$? If not, the work is done, the alternating series $\sum (-1)^n a_n$ must be diverging (D).

However if $\lim_{n\to\infty} a_n = 0$, there is no conclusion yet, and you must go to the third step.

"Step 3: For large n only, do we have $a_{n+1} < a_n$? You may ignore many terms at the beginning. If for large n we always have $a_{n+1} < a_n$, then the original alternating series is conditionally converging (AC), otherwise it is diverging (D). The whole question is done now.

"The process can be expressed by a flow chart as following. Go step by step (like guided by a *GPS*) according to this flow chart, you can certainly reach the answer (converging or diverging) for the alternating series."

The following flow chart helps Ophelia and friends to study alternating series.

[1] Is $\sum a_n$ C or D? (yes or no?)

$$\left\{ \begin{array}{l} yes \to AC \\ \\ \\ no \to [2]\lim_{n\to\infty} a_n = 0? \left\{ \begin{array}{l} no \to D \\ yes \to [3]a_{n+1} < a_n? \left\{ \begin{array}{l} yes \to CC \\ no \to D \end{array} \right. \end{array} \right. \end{array} \right.$$

Chapter 12
Functions and Graphs

12.1 A way to decide polynomial coefficients

Dr.C asked his students a question that seemed to be very hard. "There is a fourth order polynomial $f(x) = ax^4 + bx^3 + cx^2 + dx + e$. When x is 0, 1, 2, 3, 4, $f(x)$ is 6, −4, −60, −252, −718 respectively. Please find all five coefficients a, b, c, d, e."

Was this a solvable question? Yes, it was solvable. Several students already started the calculation. They substituted the five pair (x, y) values into the equation, got five coupled linear equations, then tried to solve the coupled linear equations by substitution, elimination, Cramer's rule or other methods.

For instance $f(4) = a(4^4) + b(4^3) + c(4^2) + d(4) + e = -718$, (or $256a^4 + 64b + 16c + 4d + e = -718$). The five equations were:

$$e = 6$$
$$a + b + c + d + e = -4$$
$$16a + 8b + 4c + 2d + e = -60$$
$$81a + 27b + 9c + 3d + e = -252$$
$$256a^4 + 64b + 16c + 4d + e = -718$$

Ten minutes passed. This question took so long to be solved and it was easy to make a mistake. The students looked at Dr.C, hoped to have a simpler method to do it.

Dr.C said: "When the five given x values are consecutive, like 7, 8, 9, 10, 11, or 1, 2, 3, 4, 5, we may try another approach --- solve it by finite difference. Finite difference gives us the results in Table 1:

Table 1

x	f(x)	$\Delta_1 y$	$\Delta_2 y$	$\Delta_3 y$	$\Delta_4 y$
0	6				
1	−4	−10			
2	−60	−56	−46		
3	−252	−192	−136	−90	
4	−718	−466	−274	−138	−48

"For example, $(-4)-(6) = -10$, $(-60)-(-4) = -56$, and so on. Only the top cell of each column is useful, that is, 6, -10, -46, -90 and -48. Next, do the same finite difference from the general expression of the equation $f(x) = ax^4 + bx^3 + cx^2 + dx + e$. The results are shown in Table 2. In order to be clear, we only show the top cell values in the table below.

"Compare the two tables, we have

$$e = 6$$
$$a + b + c + d = -10$$
$$14a + 6b + 2c = -46$$
$$36a + 6b = -90$$
$$24a = -48$$

196

Table 2

x	$f(x)$	$\Delta_1 y$	$\Delta_2 y$	$\Delta_3 y$	$\Delta_4 y$
0	e				
1	$a+b+c+d+e$	$a+b+c+d$			
2	$16a+8b+4c$ $+2d+e$	......	$14a+6b+2c$		
3	$81a+27b$ $+9c+3d+e$	......	......	$36a+6b$	
4	$256a+64b$ $+16c+4d+e$	......	......	......	$24a$

"Please do not think that we got another group of five coupled linear equations again. Actually this time it is quite different. Compare the two tables we know a and e immediately. The number -48 in the first table is at the same position as the $24a$ in the second table, therefore $24a = -48$ and $a = -2$. Similarly we have $e = 6$. The fourth equation gives us $36a + 6b = -90$, since $a = -2$ we know that $b = -3$. The third equation leads to $c = 0$, and finally the second equation produces $d = -5$. The original polynomial is therefore $f(x) = -2x^4 - 3x^3 - 5x + 6$."

At the end of the class Dr.C told the students: "I hope this example can open your eyes wider. A math problem can often be solved from different angles. In many cases the way to solve a problem is not unique."

12.2 Numbers and functions, odd or even?

During the study of odd functions and even functions, the students remembered what they had learned about odd numbers and even numbers in the early days. Naturally they would like to compare these concepts and aspects. Pam and friends asked Dr.C: "When we talk about odd or even functions, is the theory similar to that of odd and even numbers? If not, what are the differences?" These topics were not found in textbooks, usually not taught by teachers.

"Don't worry", said Dr.C, "let us compare numbers with functions thoroughly and systematically.

"A function is called an odd function if $f(-x) = -f(x)$; if $f(-x) = f(x)$ it is an even function. Odd functions are symmetric to the origin, while even functions are symmetric to the y-axis. Not every function can be classified as odd or even; many of them are neither odd nor even, like $f(x) = x - 3$.

"An odd function changes its sign when x is changed to $-x$. An even function does not change its sign when x is changed to $-x$. For the function $y = x^n$, it is even if n is an even number; it is odd if n is an odd number. So the simplest case of an odd function is $y = x$ or $y = x^3$; while the simplest case of an even function is $y = x^2$ or $y = x^4$. However, if you conclude that odd or even functions must be in $y = x^n$ form then you are wrong. A function such as $y = 3\sin x - 8\tan x$ or $y = e^x - e^{-x}$ is odd; while a function like $y = 5\cos x$ or $y = |3x|$ is even.

"Because $y = x^n$ is an odd function when n is an odd number; and an even function when n is an even number; people might think that functions and numbers follow the same rules. Indeed there are fundamental differences. For example an odd number times an odd number the result is still odd ($3 \times 5 = 15$), but an odd function multiplied by another odd function, the result is an even function ($x^3 \cdot x^5 = x^8$, or $x^3 \cdot \sin x = (-x)^3 \sin(-x)$).

"Well, let us study this in more details. In the example of $x^3 \cdot x^5 = x^8$, both 3 and 5 are exponents. Remind that exponents follow the rule $x^m \cdot x^n = x^{m+n}$. Odd number 3 plus odd number 5, the result 8 is even. In the other example $x^3 \cdot \sin x = (-x)^3 \sin(-x)$, under the Taylor expansion every term of $\sin x$ is an odd exponent of x, therefore it still follows the rule of exponential calculation."

Dr.C drew a table (see below) to compare odd/even numbers and odd/even functions. In the table N stands for 'neither' (not odd, not even, example $y = x + 1$). Dr.C pointed out: "The 'N' cases are more complicated, because N+N could yield any result, such as $\dfrac{1}{2} + \dfrac{1}{2} = 1$, $\dfrac{1}{2} + \dfrac{3}{2} = 2$, $\dfrac{1}{2} + \dfrac{4}{3} = \dfrac{11}{6}$ (odd, even, or neither). Functions N+N could produce an odd function like $(x^3 - 1) + (x^3 + 1) = 2x^3$, or an even function $(x - 1) + (x^2 - x + 1) = x^2$, or could be another N case such as in $(x^3 - 2) + (x^3 + 1) = 2x^3 - 1$.

Dr.C said: "You do not need to remember every detail in this table; all conclusions can be easily derived from simple examples. What we need to do is really understand the nature of math: Exponents calculations convert multiplication to addition, so that the multiplication of functions actually follows the same rule as the addition of numbers."

		Odd / even numbers	Odd / even functions	
+	O+O=E	(3+5=8)	O+O=O $(x^3 + x^5)$	
+	O+E=O	(3+2=5)	O+E=N $(x^3 + x^2)$	
+	E+O=O	(2+3=5)	E+O=N $(x^4 + x^3)$	
+	E+E=E	(2+4=6)	E+E=E $(x^4 + x^2)$	Same
×	O×O=O	(3×1=3)	O×O=E $(x^3 \cdot x^7 = x^{10})$	
×	O×E=E	(3×2=6)	O×E=O $(x^3 \cdot x^2 = x^5)$	
×	E×O=E	(2×3=6)	E×O=O $(x^2 \cdot x^3 = x^5)$	
×	E×E=E	(2×4=8)	E×E=E $(x^2 \cdot x^4 = x^6)$	Same
÷	O÷O=O or N	(9÷3, 11÷3)	O÷O=E $(x^5 \div x^3 = x^2)$	
÷	O÷E=N	(5÷2)	O÷E=O $(x^5 \div (x^2 - 1))$	
÷	E÷O=E or N	(6÷3, 6÷5)	E÷O=O $(x^4 \div x^3 = x)$	
÷	E÷E=O, E, or N	(6÷2, 8÷2, 8÷6)	E÷E=E $(x^4 \div x^6 = x^{-2})$	

The last column compared the rules for numbers with the rules for functions (same or not the same, empty means not the same).

12.3 "Domain is easy, range is hard"? --- Think again!

Today two opinions emerged from Dr.C's math class. Some students thought that the domain of a function was easy; the range of a function was hard. Others held an opposite opinion --- they said: "domain is hard and range is easy". Both sides insisted that they had their reasons and examples.

Linda and Eugene insisted "domain is easy, range is hard". Eugene said: "It is not difficult to find the domain of a function --- just see where the function is *undefined*. The denominator of a fraction cannot be zero; the inside of a square root cannot be negative, etc. Exclude those 'bad' places, the rest is the domain. Therefore the domain of function $f(x) = \sqrt{x-1}$ is $x \geq 1$, written as $D\{x \in R \mid x \geq 1\}$, while the domain of function $f(x) = \dfrac{1}{100 - x^2}$ is $x^2 \neq 100$, written as $D\{x \in R \mid x \neq \pm 10\}$; simple!"

Linda said: "Why do we say that the range of a function is hard to determine? Please see the above example $f(x) = \dfrac{1}{100 - x^2}$. This function can be positive (example; when $x = 1$); can be negative (example; $x = 11$); but cannot be zero since the numerator is not zero. From here we may write its range as $R\{y \in R \mid y \neq 0\}$. Is this range correct? No! We know that the function $y = 100 - x^2$ is a parabola that opens downward. If we draw $y = 100 - x^2$ together with its reciprocal $y = \dfrac{1}{100 - x^2}$, we may find that its correct range is nothing but $R\{y \in R \mid -\infty < y < 0, \ 0.01 \leq y < \infty\}$. In a *very narrow* region $0 \leq y < 0.01$, the function is undefined."

"This example is excellent," commented Dr.C. "Because the undefined region is so narrow, it is very easy to be ignored. If you only try some test values you may find that $y = \pm 1$, $\pm 2...$, all are possible, then you may think that only $y = 0$ is impossible. Indeed there exists a very narrow hidden region where the function is forbidden. That region $0 \le y < 0.01$ is too small to be shown in a scaled diagram. Hence we draw another diagram. In the following diagram the solid curve is $f(x) = 2 - x^2$, its reciprocal is

$f(x) = \dfrac{1}{2 - x^2}$ (shown as the dotted curve). The domain of this dotted

curve is $(x \in R \mid x \ne \pm\sqrt{2})$, whereas its range is $(y \in R \mid y \ge \frac{1}{2}$, $y < 0)$.

If we come back to $f(x) = \dfrac{1}{100 - x^2}$, such an impossible region would

change from $(0 \le y < \frac{1}{2})$ to $(0 \le y < \frac{1}{100})$ and would be hard to show. You

can imagine the diagram of $f(x) = \dfrac{1}{100 - x^2}$ from the diagram below."

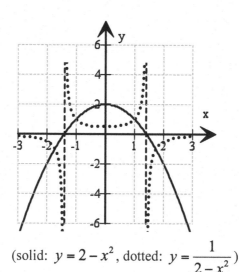

(solid: $y = 2 - x^2$, dotted: $y = \dfrac{1}{2 - x^2}$)

202

John and Barbara said: "Dr.C, we also have our examples to show that domain is hard and range is easy. Just look at the function $f(x) = \sqrt{\dfrac{(x-4)(x+3)}{(x+7)(x+6)}}$. The range of this function is easy: $R\{y \in R \mid y \geq 0\}$ because a square root cannot be negative. However, what is its domain? What x guarantees that the function is defined?"

Dr.C said: "This example is also excellent. In this example let us call the inside of the square root $g(x)$, so $g(x) = \dfrac{(x-4)(x+3)}{(x+7)(x+6)}$. How can this function be non-negative? It is undefined at $x = -7$ and -6. It is 0 when $x = 4$ or -3. Hence there are four special points $x = -7, -6, -3$, and 4. These four points divide the number axis into 5 sections.

	-7	-6	-3	4
x axis				$\longrightarrow$
$(x-4)$	$-$	$-$	$-$	$-$	$+$
$(x+3)$	$-$	$-$	$-$	$+$	$+$
$(x+6)$	$-$	$-$	$+$	$+$	$+$
$(x+7)$	$-$	$+$	$+$	$+$	$+$
$g(x)$	$+$	$-$	$+$	$-$	$+$

"Now we see where $g(x) > 0$ (the three regions with + signs). Therefore the domain of the original function $f(x) = \sqrt{\dfrac{(x-4)(x+3)}{(x+7)(x+6)}}$ is $D\{x \in R \mid x < -7, \ -6 < x \leq -3, \text{ and } x \geq 4\}$.

"The examples discussed today show that both the domain and the range of a relation could be complicated and could be easy. We should learn the method to find the domain in this example, and remember the method we used to find the hidden range in the previous question."

Finally Dr.C pointed out: "When you determine the domain of a relation, be aware that you should not simplify the function first then find its domain. For instance the function $f(x) = \dfrac{x(x-2)}{(x+3)(x-2)}$ can be simplified

as $f(x) = \dfrac{x}{x+3}$ (cancel the common part $(x-2)$). You might feel that the domain is $x \neq -3$. Actually the domain of the original function is $D\{x \in R \mid x \neq 2, x \neq -3\}$. The two points are different in nature: $x = 2$ is a hole, while $x = -3$ is a vertical asymptote."

12.4 Order of transformations

Tony and Monica have just learned transformations of functions and relations. The hard part is to master the order of transformations when more than one transformation is required. They discussed this topic with Dr.C.

Monica said: "Dr,C, we just learned various basic transforms of functions and relations. We understand each of them individually. For instance when $y = f(x)$ is changed to $y = f(x)+1$ the curve moves up 1 step. Similarly we have $y = f(x)-1$ (down 1), $y = f(x-1)$ (right 1), $y = f(x+1)$ (left 1), etc. If $f(x)$ is changed into $2f(x)$ we multiply the y value by 2 (vertically stretch by a factor of 2), whereas if $f(x)$ is changed into $f(2x)$, it is under a horizontal compression, where the x value is changed to $\dfrac{1}{2}x$ and the y value is untouched."

"However," asked Tony, "if we have two or more transformations, for example from $y = f(x)$ to $y = 2f(2x)$, which transformation should be done first?"

Dr.C answered: "From $y = f(x)$ to $y = 2f(2x)$, you may do whichever first. Because x and y are independent, you can either do x first or do y first. Assume that the original function has a point (2, 3), then to change x first you will get (1, 3) in the first step, next to change y so that (1, 3) becomes (1, 6). On the other hand if you change y first, (2, 3) will become (2, 6), then change x and (2, 6) becomes (1, 6). The final answers are the same.

"However, if you want to change $y = f(x)$ into $y = 2f(x)+1$, the order cannot be reversed. Again assume that $y = f(x)$ has a point (2, 3), then adding 1 to y the point becomes (2, 4). Multiply the y value by 2 and the final answer will be (2, 8) (*incorrect*). The correct way is to multiply y by 2 first so that (2, 3) becomes (2, 6), then add 1 to the y value so the final answer is (2, 7) (correct).

"As a summary: for x we should do multiplication and division before we do addition and subtraction. For y we should also do multiplication and division before we do addition and subtraction. As to x and y, there is no requirement, you can do either one first. If we consider multiplication and division as priority 1, consider addition and subtraction as priority 2, then orders like $x1, x2, y1, y2$ or $y1, x1, y2, x2$ are correct. As long as for either x or y the operation 1 is before the operation 2, then that order is correct. We don't compare x operations with y operations."

Monica asked: "Dr.C, can we apply this rule to a longer expression? What is the correct order to change $y = f(x)$ to $y = \frac{1}{5}f(\frac{1}{2}(x+3))-1$?"

Dr.C answered: "Certainly we can apply exact the same rules as stated above to more complicated questions. However, I would like to tell you a tip, a smart and easy tip. When a function is written in this form (like $y = \frac{1}{5} f(\frac{1}{2}(x+3)) - 1$), you may simply go from left to right.

"In this example, going from left to right means first $y \div 5$, then $x \times 2$, then $x - 3$, finally $y - 1$. Assume the original function has a point (5, 20), then we will have these points in order: (5, 4), (10, 4), (7, 4), and finally (7, 3).

"This simple way (from left to right), agrees with the rules stated above ($y1, x1, x2, y2$). For x 1 is before 2; for y 1 is also before 2. There is no relation between y and x, you don't have to finish y then do x."

"But be aware," said Dr.C. "If this function is originally written as $y = -1 + \frac{1}{5} f(\frac{1}{2}(x+3))$, it is the same function as above, but this time you cannot go from left to right. Another example is in trigonometry most times we write $y = -2\sin(3(\theta + 60°)) - 1$ instead of $y = -1 - 2\sin(3(\theta + 60°))$, although both expressions are identical. If a function is written in the 'normal way' $y = -2\sin(3(\theta + 60°)) - 1$, you may go from left to right. Otherwise, consider order of operations (doing $\times, \div$ before doing $+, -$)."

Monica and Tony learned the method taught by Dr.C. "**For x, do $\times$, $\div$ before $+, -$;   For y, do $\times, \div$ before $+, -$. No relation between x and y. If the expression is written in 'normal' order, go from left to right with caution.**"

"Easy!" said Monica and Tony. "Thank you. You always teach us the simplest methods not found in textbooks nor taught in our schools."

Dr.C said: "Now you have learned the basic functions and the basic relations (linear, quadratic, cubic, reciprocal, absolute value, circles, square roots, trigonometric functions) and their graphs; you also understand order of transformations. You are ready to learn calculus."

12.5 What function equals its own inverse?

Inverse function $f^{-1}(x)$ reverses the relationship between x and y. If $(2,-5)$ is a point of the original function, then the corresponding point of the inverse function is $(-5,2)$. How can we find the inverse of a given function? Use the two-step method.

Step 1: Exchange x and y. Do not change the structure of the function. For instance, we change the function $y = \dfrac{2x-9}{4}$ to $x = \dfrac{2y-9}{4}$.

Step 2: Solve the new y. In this example $x = \dfrac{2y-9}{4}$ means $4x = 2y - 9$, so that $f^{-1}(x) = y = 2x + \dfrac{9}{2}$.

The inverse function of a function may or may not be a function.

In today's class Dr.C asked the students a special question: "What type of function is the same as its own inverse?"

Hans answered immediately: "I know, that is $y = x$. If A equals B, then B equals A."

Judy said: "And $y = \dfrac{1}{x}$. If $y = \dfrac{1}{x}$ then $x = \dfrac{1}{y}$."

Dr.C smiled: "I am glad that Judy and Hans answered quickly and correctly. More complicated functions could also be the same as their inverses. Please find the inverse of $f(x) = \dfrac{4x+9}{5x-4}$."

Students applied the two-step method, the answer was $f^{-1}(x) = f(x) = \dfrac{4x+9}{5x-4}$, exactly the same as the given function.

Dr.C drew the sketch of this function on the board. The diagram was *symmetric* to the line $y = x$ (see below). Any function symmetric to the line $y = x$ is the same as its inverse.

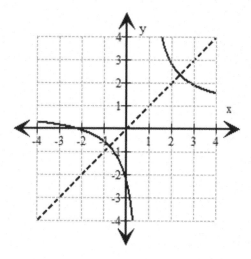

$$f^{-1}(x) = f(x) = \dfrac{4x+9}{5x-4}$$

"Whatever the coefficients a, b and c are," said Dr.C. "The function $y = \dfrac{ax+b}{cx-a}$ is *always* the same as its own inverse, as long as in the expression a appears twice with opposite signs. For example, $y = \dfrac{7x-8}{4x-7}$ and $y = \dfrac{-2x+3}{11x+2}$ satisfy the requirement, but $y = \dfrac{-2x+3}{11x-2}$ does not.

"Such a logic can be extended into the discussion of composite functions. Under what situation do we have $f(g(x)) = g(f(x))$? Of course the simple answer is when $f(x) = g(x)$. Even if $f(x) \neq g(x)$ we can still have $f(g(x)) = g(f(x))$. Examples: $f(x) = \dfrac{1}{3}x + 9$ and $g(x) = 3x - 27$. It is easy to prove that $f(g(x)) = g(f(x))$ in this case."

Dr.C continued: "I would like to remind you that the inverse function is not the same as the reciprocal function $y = \dfrac{1}{f(x)}$. While the inverse of a function changes (x, y) into (y, x), the reciprocal function changes (x, y) into $(x, \frac{1}{y})$."

12.6 The behavior of quadratic and cubic points

Donna told Dr.C: "We have just learned how to sketch the graph of a function. For example $f(x) = x(x-1)^2(x+2)^3$ is a polynomial function, it has 3 zeroes: 0, 1 and -2. The three points look different on the graph. At

$x = 0$ the curve simply intersects the coordinate axis. At $x = 1$ it only touches the x-axis, does not intersect it. At $x = -2$ the curve crosses the x-axis in a special way --- the curve is distorted. Why do they behave so differently?"

The curve of $f(x) = x(x-1)^2(x+2)^3$ looks like this:

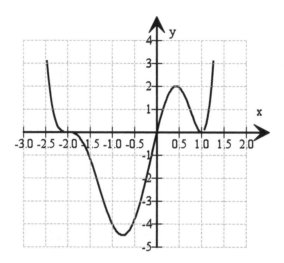

Dr.C said: "Let me explain --- you may judge whether I am right or wrong. The polynomial $y = (x-1)^2$ has only one zero $x = 1$, and no region below the x-axis. If we change $y = (x-1)^2$ to $y = (x-0.999)(x-1.001)$, it will cross the x-coordinate at two zeroes 0.999 and 1.001. When the two zeroes approach each other, they will merge and become one point at $x = 1$. Before they merge the curve crosses over the x axis a little bit, after the merge, the curve merely touch the x axis.

"Next, study the curve $f(x) = (x+1.999)(x+2)(x+2.001)$, it is a cubic curve with three zeroes very closely distributed: -1.999, -2.000 and -2.001. Magnifying the diagram we get the following figure. Then imagine that the left zero and the right zero squeeze to the middle, then we get the curve of $y = (x + 2)(x + 2)(x + 2)$, which is $y = (x + 2)^3$. The curve $y = (x + 2)^3$ still crosses the x-axis but with a zigzag, a remnant from typical cubic curves."

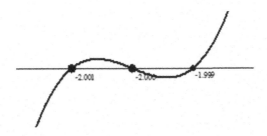

After squeezing:

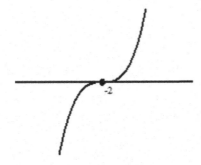

Since the students already had a thorough knowledge of the graph of functions, it was easy for them to understand the curve obtained by squeezing towards the middle. This way of creative teaching inspired Donna and other students and prepared them for further study of math --- the concept of *limits* in calculus.

12.7 Can a curve intersect its own asymptotes?

Mary said: "A curve can only approach its own asymptotes indefinitely, but cannot intersect it. The word 'asymptote' itself means that the function is undefined there, if a curve can meet its own asymptote, it is then defined at that point, and that is ridiculous".

Students discussed Mary's point, some agreed, others disagreed. Nana was one of the latter. Dr.C encouraged Nana to teach this lesson. He himself sat among the students.

Nana said: "What Mary said is only half true. Any curve cannot intersect its own *vertical* asymptote. In fact in order to locate the vertical asymptotes, just let the denominator of a rational function be zero --- be aware of possible 'holes'. For example, $x = 1$ is a hole on the curve $f(x) = \dfrac{(x-1)(x-3)}{(x-1)(x-2)}$. If $x \neq 1$ we can cancel $(x-1)$ from the numerator and the denominator, get $f(x) = \dfrac{(x-3)}{(x-2)}$. However these two functions are different, the second one x can equal to 1 but the first one cannot. Except that the two functions are the same. The function $f(x) = \dfrac{(x-1)(x-3)}{(x-1)(x-2)}$ is undefined at $x = 1$ (a hole) and $x = 2$ (a vertical asymptote with $\lim_{x \to 2^-} f(x) = \infty$ and $\lim_{x \to 2^+} f(x) = -\infty$). Any curve cannot intersect its own vertical asymptotes.

"However, horizontal or oblique asymptotes maybe (or may not be) intersected by the curve. Because they are only defined at $x \to \infty$ and at $x \to -\infty$, it is allowed to cross a horizontal or an oblique asymptote line at any finite value of x."

Mary said: "Nana, can you show us an example?"

"Sure," Nana sketched the diagram of function $f(x) = \dfrac{x^2 + 2}{x(x+3)}$ as below.

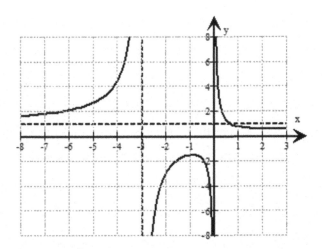

"Either from the calculation or just by viewing the diagram, we know that the horizontal asymptote of the curve $f(x) = \dfrac{x^2 + 2}{x(x+3)}$ is $f(x) = 1$. Since $f(\frac{2}{3}) = 1$ and $f(0.5) > 1$, $f(1) < 1$, the function intersects its own horizontal asymptote $f(x) = 1$ at $x = \dfrac{2}{3}$. On the other hand the function is undefined at both $x = 0$ and $x = -3$, and the curve cannot intersect its vertical asymptotes at those places."

Mary and classmates applauded to accept Nana's explanation.

Nana continued: "Because we learned vertical asymptotes first, we might get the idea that 'asymptotes cannot be intersected', which turned out to be *not always* true. In order to sketch a curve, if there is a vertical asymptote we may choose two points near the vertical line, one on each side. We only need to check the sign (+ or −), not the function value there. In the above example $f(-3.1) > 0$ and $f(-2.9) < 0$, so that the function approaches positive infinity on the left side of $x = -3$, and approaches negative infinity on the right side of $x = -3$.

"Nevertheless, to the horizontal asymptote $y = 1$, only knowing the sign (+ or −) of $f(x)$ at $x \to \infty$ and $x \to -\infty$ is *not enough*. We must really find the function values at two sample places and compare them with the horizontal asymptote. For example $f(100) = 0.97 < 1$ and $f(-100) = 1.03 > 1$, so that the curve lies below the horizontal asymptote and approaches it from below when $x \to \infty$; and lies above the horizontal asymptote and approaches it from above when $x \to -\infty$. Adding special points like the x and y intercepts, the curve can be sketched."

"Excellent!" said Dr.C. "To understand that a curve can intersect its own horizontal or oblique asymptotes is important. Let us sketch the function $f(x) = \dfrac{-(x-2)(3x+2)}{x^2}$. Its V.A is $x = 0$, the function approaches positive infinity from both sides of $x = 0$. Its H.A is $y = -3$. The function has x intercepts $-\dfrac{2}{3}$ and 2. If we only rely on these pieces of information we might sketch a *wrong* diagram like the one below (The dotted part of the diagram is *incorrect*).

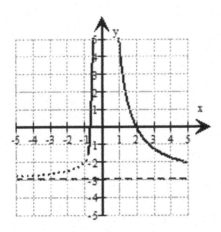

"Try to calculate the function values at $x = 100$ and $x = -100$, the results are $f(100) = -2.96 > -3$ (above the horizontal asymptote) and $f(-100) = -3.04 < -3$ (below it). Therefore in the above diagram, behavior of the function when $x \to -\infty$ must be incorrect. The correct curve is shown in the following diagram. The difference here is that, now we accept the idea that a curve can intersect its own horizontal asymptotes."

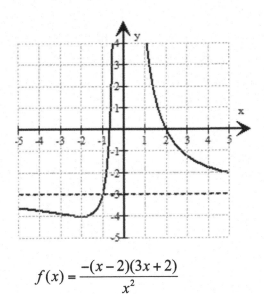

$$f(x) = \frac{-(x-2)(3x+2)}{x^2}$$

Finally Dr.C said: "The above method to sketch a curve is only qualitative. To be more accurate we need to consider a complete algorithm which can be found in calculus textbooks (domain, intercepts, symmetry, asymptotes, increasing and decreasing, local maxima and minima, points of inflection, concave up and concave down, etc.). Since you will learn these in your school, I am not going to talk about them today."

12.8 A thorough discussion on ellipses and hyperbolas

Dr.C always tries to give lectures thoroughly. He writes the following equation on the white board:

$$\frac{x^2}{16} + \frac{y^2}{9} = 1$$

Dr.C asks several questions about this ellipse equation. "(a) Write down the coordinates of the x and y intercepts, (b) where are the foci of this ellipse? (c) Write down the equations of the axes of symmetry, and (d) what are the domain and the range of this ellipse?"

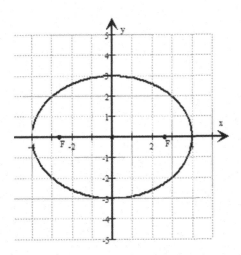

Well, such questions are not hard. The answers are : (a) $(\pm 4, 0)$, $(0, \pm 3)$, totally 4 points; (b) $(\pm\sqrt{7}, 0)$, two points; (c) the major axis of symmetry is along the x axis $(y = 0)$; and the minor axis is along the y axis $(x = 0)$, and (d) with the domain $(x \in R \mid -4 \leq x \leq 4)$ and the range $(y \in R \mid -3 \leq y \leq 3)$.

Dr.C further asks the students what would be the difference if we change the right side from 1 to -1. Do we need to revise the above answers or can keep them?

Amy says that such a change would make the equation non-solvable, since the square of a real number cannot be negative. Obviously she is right.

"What happens if the right side becomes 0?"

"The curve now shrinks to a point (the origin $(0, 0)$)," answered Simon. "Both its domain and its range become just $x = 0$ and $y = 0$."

"What happens if the equation becomes $\dfrac{x^2}{16} - \dfrac{y^2}{9} = 1$?"

Tina and Hans reply: "This time the curve is a hyperbola, it looks very different from an ellipse. A hyperbola only intersects one coordinate axis. In this problem they meet the x-axis at $(4,0)$ and $(-4,0)$. The foci are $(\pm 5,0)$ on the x-axis. There is no intersection point on the y axis. The domain is D $(x \in R \,|\, x \le -4 \text{ or } x \ge 4)$ and the range now is R $(y \in R)$, any y value is possible."

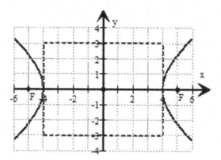

"Right, but what would happen if we switch the numbers 16 with 9, so that the hyperbola equation $\dfrac{x^2}{16} - \dfrac{y^2}{9} = 1$ becomes $\dfrac{x^2}{9} - \dfrac{y^2}{16} = 1$?" asks Dr.C.

Harry answers: "It is still a horizontal hyperbola. As to the answer of the four questions, (a) the curve $\dfrac{x^2}{9} - \dfrac{y^2}{16} = 1$ meets the x-axis at $(3,0)$ and $(-3,0)$. The foci are the same as answered by Tina and Hans $(\pm 5,0)$. The curve passes the x-axis only, not the y-axis, with a domain D $(x \in R \,|\, x \le -3$ or $x \ge 3)$ and a range R $(y \in R)$."

"Excellent. What is the situation if the equation becomes

$$\frac{x^2}{16} - \frac{y^2}{9} = -1?"$$

Well, after a debate everybody agrees that the equation is still a hyperbola but now with the intersection points $(0,3)$ and $(0,-3)$. Its foci $(0,\pm5)$ are on the y-axis now. A vertical hyperbola intersects the y-axis, not the x-axis. In this question the domain is $(x \in R)$ and the range is $(y \in R \mid y \le -3$ or $y \ge 3)$.

Dr.C continues: "If the center of the ellipse $\frac{x^2}{16} + \frac{y^2}{9} = 1$ moves to $(-2,4)$, what happens to the equation and to the answers of the above four questions?"

Peter: "The equation becomes $\frac{(x+2)^2}{16} + \frac{(y-4)^2}{9} = 1$."

Anny says: "Now the curve does not intersect the x-axis, it intersects the y-axis at $(0,6.6)$ and $(0,1.4)$. These numbers can be found by substituting 0 as x in the equation."

Tom says: "The focus points now become $(-2+\sqrt{7},4)$ and $(-2-\sqrt{7},4)$."

Elisabeth says: "$x = -2$ and $y = 4$ are the symmetric axes now."

Andrew says: "The domain is $(x \in R \mid -6 \le x \le 2)$, and the range is $(y \in R \mid 1 \le y \le 7)$ now."

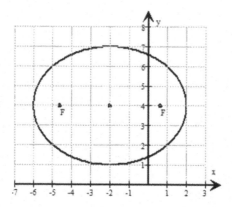

These answers are all correct.

Dr.C does not want to stop there. He further discusses equations

$$\frac{(x+2)^2}{9} + \frac{(y-4)^2}{16} = 1,$$

$$\frac{(x+2)^2}{16} - \frac{(y-4)^2}{9} = -1,$$

$$\frac{(x+2)^2}{16} - \frac{(y-4)^2}{9} = 1, \text{ and more.}$$

As a conclusion, Dr.C says: "Very good, we discussed many questions today. It is always a good idea to go deeper into a topic, ask ourselves more questions and study the subject thoroughly. There was a popular science book with the title '*One hundred thousand whys*'. As suggested by that book, we should ask ourselves again and again, 5000 '*where*'s, ten thousand '*how*'s, and one hundred thousand '*why*'s. My friends, let us remember the famous statement: '*In the world, there are always one hundred thousand whys.*'"

12.9 Does logarithm change fast or slow?

"Why is logarithm useful? Because it has two features, both slow and fast." said Dr.C.

Students were surprised: "How can it be both slow and fast at the same time?"

Dr.C explained the "slow" feature first: "When a number increases from 1 to one million, its common logarithm $\log_{10} x$ (or simply $\log x$) changes only from 1 to 6. This slow change makes it quite useful. In a x -- $\log y$ graph, both large numbers and small numbers can be shown clearly. You do not lose small number details when you see big numbers. On the other hand for a non-logarithm function $y = x$ when x changes from 1 to 1000000, y also changes from 1 to 1000000. A graph of x --- y would lose all details near small numbers (y = 1, 2, 3, etc). When x approaches to infinity, $y = \log x$ also approaches to infinity but at a much slower pace.

"Logarithms convert large numbers to small numbers, therefore make calculations easy. It works so effectively. We know that the most elementary operations are addition and subtraction. The second level operations are multiplication and division. The third level operations are powers and roots. The advantage of using logarithm in calculation is to reduce the operation by one level. Logarithms change multiplication and division to addition and subtraction, change power to multiplication, roots to divisions, thus lower the operation by one level and greatly simplify the calculation. We know, an addition (like $7586 + 3497$) is much simpler and easier than a multiplication (like 7586×3497).

"Logarithm reduces the operation by one level. What is the advantage of this change? It changes 'slow' to 'fast'! Lower level operations immediately speed up the process of calculation. Without calculator it would be tedious to evaluate high exponents like this one:

$$N = \frac{(1667)^9 (24983)^{12}}{(687.34)^{13}}$$

"With logarithms we can easily convert this to an easy question $\log N = 9\log 1667 + 12\log 24983 - 13\log 687.34$, we can find $\log N$ and N quickly. Another example is to solve an equation with exponents (like $6^x = 7$). Without logarithms one can solve it by trial and error, guess and test the solutions one after another. With logarithms we can solve this kind equation directly and accurately. Exponents and logarithms form a pair. Logarithm played an important role in speeding up calculations before the invention of modern calculators. Even today it is still a must-have tool in mathematics."

12.10 Too many solutions? Too few solutions?

Dr.C said: "Sometimes it is not enough to find just one solution, we need more. Sometimes we refuse more solutions, just accept one. Sometimes even one solution is too many; there should be no solution at all for a given question.

"Let us start with a junior level math question. If Shirley and Vivian together have 5 apples, Peter and Vivian together have 6 apples, Donna and Peter together have 4 apples, then how many apples do Shirley and Donna together have? Does this question have only one answer, or more than one?

"Well, there is only one answer: 3 apples. Because (Shirley and Vivian)+(Donna and Peter), all four together have 5+4 = 9 apples. Among the 9, Peter and Vivian have 6 together, so the rest 3 belong to Shirley and Donna. This question has only one solution.

"If we change the question to the following: Shirley and Vivian together have 5 apples, Peter and Donna together have 6 apples, then how many apples do Peter and Shirley have together? This time the answer is not unique. For example (Shirley 1, Vivian 4, Peter 4, Donna 2, so Peter +Shirley = 5) and (Shirley 3, Vivian 2, Peter 1, Donna 5, so Peter +Shirley = 4) are both possible. In this case one solution is too few. There are 12 answers (0, 1, 2, up to 11) available (we only consider whole numbers, not fraction or decimal). Shirley may have 0 to 5 apples, Peter may have 0 to 6 apples, their sum can be as small as 0 (0 + 0), or as large as 11 (5 + 6), together 12 possible answers.

"Another example is to calculate the square roots. If you solve the equation $x^2 = 26.7289$, your calculator tells you that $x = 5.17$, however, one solution is too few, there is a hidden solution $x = -5.17$, don't forget that.

"Let us study the following geometry question. Given three of the four vertices of a parallelogram, please locate the fourth vertex. If the given vertices are A(1, 0), B(4, 0) and C(5, 2), then possible answers of the fourth vertex could be D(2, 2), E(0, −2), or F(8, 2) . The parallelogram could be $\square ABCD$, $\square AEBC$, or $\square ABFC$.

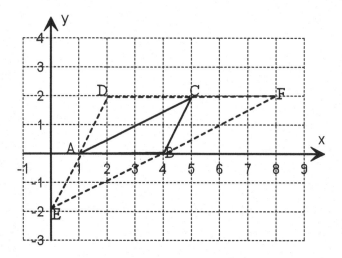

"If the question says that three of the four vertices A, B, C of parallelogram $\square ABCD$ are given, find the unknown vertex D, then there is only one answer D(2, 2).   Because if we consider D as (8, 2), the parallelogram is $\square ABDC$, not $\square ABCD$. Here the order is important.

"We have talked about the ambiguous cases of the sine law.   If we solve the trigonometric equation $\sin\theta = 0.5$ where $0° \le \theta \le 360°$, a calculator gives us one answer $\theta = 30°$.   That is not enough.   There exists the second answer $\theta = 150°$.   In case of $\sin 2\theta = 0.5$ where $0° \le \theta \le 360°$, $0° \le 2\theta \le 720°$, we will have totally four solutions $15°, 75°, 195°, 255°$."

Dr.C continued to say: "Sometimes we get two or more solutions, but only accept one and discard the other(s). If we solve the equation $\sqrt{x-3} = x-5$, square both sides we get $(x-3) = (x-5)^2$.   Such a quadratic equation have two solutions $x = 4$ and $x = 7$.   Only $x = 7$ is accepted. The other solution $x = 4$ must be discarded because if $x = 4$ then $\sqrt{x-3} = x-5$ would lead to $\sqrt{1} = -1$, which is wrong.

"A similar equation $\sqrt{5x+1} = x+1$, however, does have two valid solutions $x = 0$ and $x = 3$. If $x = 0$, equation $\sqrt{5x+1} = x+1$ becomes $\sqrt{1} = 1$; if $x = 3$, the same equation becomes $\sqrt{16} = 4$. Both are correct.

"By substituting the answers back to the original equation we can figure out which one is acceptable and which one is not. Logarithmic equations may lead to extraneous solutions. The logarithmic equation $\ln(4x+5) - 2\ln x = 0$ gives us two solutions 5 and -1. But only the solution 5 is correct, because the other solution -1 leads to a negative x in $\ln x$. Using the same method it is not hard to show that the exponential equation $e^{2x} - 5e^x + 4 = 0$ has two valid solutions (0 and $\ln 4$), whereas the equation $e^{2x} - e^x - 6 = 0$ only has one valid solution $x = \ln 3$, the other answer does not exist.

"Inequalities with absolute values also may lead to wrong answers. For example $|x-2| < -6$. If $x \geq 2$ the inequality is equivalent to $x - 2 < -6$, thus $x < -4$. If $x < 2$ we have $-(x-2) < -6$ so $x > 8$. Be aware that **none of them is correct**. The original inequality does not have any solution at all! The absolute value cannot be less than 0. When you say 'if $x < 2$, then $x > 8$', it is already beyond the assumption that $x < 2$."

Finally Dr.C said: "Sometimes we discard an answer, not because it is wrong in mathematics, but because it is wrong in science or real life. The age of a person cannot be negative or a whole number in thousands. The mass of an object cannot be negative, the temperature of an object cannot be lower than the 'absolute zero' ($-273.15°C$), etc. If a problem yields a unreasonable answer we have to discard that answer."

Chapter 13
Vector, Introductory Linear Algebra

13.1 Two good ways to evaluate vector products

Students learned how to evaluate vector product (also called cross product) of two vectors. Different schools taught different methods. Students asked Dr.C: "Which method do you recommend for us to use?"

Dr.C replied: "Hundreds flowers bloom, hundreds ideas contend. Different teachers may prefer different methods. For me, I recommend two ways. One method is simple, the other method is similar to the way we evaluate determinates."

[Method 1]

"This is my favorite. It is the fastest and easiest method. Write down the first vector on top, repeat once, then write down the second vector at the bottom and repeat once. Then delete the left column and the right column. In the following example the first vector is $\vec{a} = [1, -3, 2]$ and the second vector is $\vec{b} = [-2, 4, 5]$.

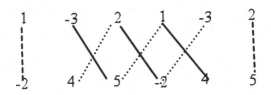

"To evaluate $\vec{a} \times \vec{b}$, the first term is $(-3)x(5)-(2)x(4)=-23$ (solid line product minus dotted line product), similarly for the other two terms. The result is $\vec{a} \times \vec{b} = [-23, -9, -2]$.

"We can also write down the two vectors vertically, then delete the top row and the bottom row, as following:

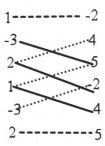

"Then we calculate terms in the same way (solid line product minus dotted line product). The result of course is the same."

[Method 2]

"This method is not the simplest one, but it reminds us of the way to evaluate 3×3 determinates. For example we write $[5, -6, -2] \times [3, 7, -4]$ as:

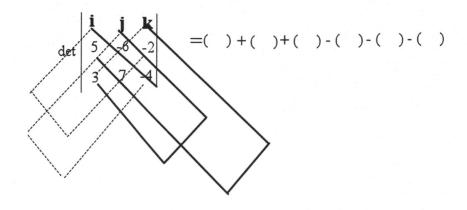

$=(\quad)+(\quad)+(\quad)-(\quad)-(\quad)-(\quad)$

228

"Learn by analogy we can write down three positive sign brackets and three negative sign brackets *before* inputting numbers (see section 8.2). Multiply the three items along each solid line and write down the results into positive brackets; multiply the three items along each dashed line and write down the results into negative brackets.

$$= (24i) +(-6j) +(35k) -(-14i) -(-20j) -(-18k)$$
$$= 24i -6j +35k +14i +20j +18k$$
$$= 38i +14j +53k$$
$$= [38, \quad 14, \quad 53]$$

"There are three ways to do vector multiplication. A number times a vector (examples: $2\vec{a}$, $-9\vec{v}$, you get a new vector parallel or anti-parallel to the original one); dot product $\vec{a} \bullet \vec{b}$ (you get a scalar); and cross product $\vec{a} \times \vec{b}$ (you get a new vector perpendicular to both given vectors)."

13.2 Teaching linear algebra by analogy

Dr.C's students like Dr.C's math classes. Unlike math classes in some schools, Dr.C teaches the course in a very interesting and inspiring way. Students feel that the class is particularly friendly. This introductory level linear algebra class is full of wonderful analogies.

[Linearly dependent or independent]

In teaching linearly dependent and independent vectors, Dr.C first introduces the definition. "If $k_1\vec{v}_1 + k_2\vec{v}_2 + k_3\vec{v}_3 + ... + k_n\vec{v}_n = \vec{0}$ where $k_1, k_2, k_3...k_n$ are not all zeroes at the same time, then $\vec{v}_1, \vec{v}_2, \vec{v}_3,...\vec{v}_n$ are linearly dependent. On the other hand if this statement only holds when all the coefficients are zeroes, then these vectors are linearly independent."

"This definition can be stated in another way: for linearly dependent vectors because not all coefficients $k_1, k_2, k_3 ... k_n$ are zeroes at the same time, we can find at least one coefficient non-zero. Dividing every term by that coefficient we can express one term as a linear combination of other terms. This task is impossible if the vectors are linearly independent."

Dr.C uses color as an example: "We know that red, blue and yellow are prime colors. It is impossible to create one of the three prime colors from the other two. Therefore red, blue and yellow are 'independent colors'. Whereas red, blue, yellow and green are dependent, because any green color can be produced by mixing yellow with blue. Green depends on yellow and blue."

[Subspace]

If V is a vector space and U is a subset of V, then U is a subspace if and only if it satisfies the following requirements: If u and w are elements of U then any linear combination of u and w is still an element of U; if u is an element of U, then ku is still an element of U where k is a scalar.

Dr.C says: "Subspace is a clearly defined concept. You may imagine that the linear space V is a big family. Some members of this large family form a smaller sub-family. These members share a common feature, we use the feature to define that subfamily. In order to be a self-closed, clearly defined concept, the sub-family must satisfy the following requirements: a member adds another member or multiplies a constant the result still possesses that defining feature. If that feature is lost during one of the two operations then the sub-family is not a subspace. For example a vectors $(1, a_2, a_3, ... a_n)$ adds another vector $(1, b_2, b_3, ... b_n)$, the result is $(2, ...)$ so that $(1, a_2, a_3, \ldots a_n)$ does not form a subspace of the n-D vector space. If we change the 1 to 0, it is a subspace."

[Span and basis]

If any vector in a subspace can be obtained by a linear combination of vectors $(v_1, v_2, v_3, \ldots v_n)$, we say $(v_1, v_2, v_3, \ldots v_n)$ span that linear subspace. In order to distinguish between span and basis, Dr.C uses an analogy: "Assume that we find a team to build a house. If the team can do the job we say that they 'span' the job. However, is everyone in that team necessary? Maybe not. Some people in that team may not be necessary. Exclude all unnecessary people, the rest is a 'basis'. Everyone in the 'basis' must be there in order to build the house. A 'basis' can build a house. A 'basis' plus more people can still build that house, but they no longer form a 'basis'."

"Red, blue and yellow colors form a basis because any other color can be obtained from a certain combination of them. A combination of yellow, blue, red and green can also 'span' any color, but this team is not a 'basis' since among the four, green is not needed."

["Hard vectors, soft vectors"]

If all members of a group of vectors are linearly independent to each other, then it is impossible to produce one member by any linear combination of other members. Dr.C says that in such a case he would call the vectors as "hard vectors" (therefore $(1, -3)$ and $(-2, -7)$ are hard vectors). In n dimension space n linearly independent vectors form a basis. In any basis every vector is hard (a "must have" member). As to vectors $(1, -3)$, $(-2, -7)$ and $(2, 7)$; though these three vectors can still span the space of all 2-D vectors, they do not form a basis since $(-2, -7)$ and $(2, 7)$ are linearly dependent. In that case we may view one of these two vectors as a "soft vector". Once all soft vectors are removed, vectors leftover are "hard" vectors only. They not only span the subspace, but also form a basis. Among the colors of red, yellow, blue and green, three of them (red, yellow, blue) are "hard colors", one (the green color) is a soft member because it can be obtained by "linear combination" of the basic prime colors.

The rank of a matrix is the number of hard vectors in it. Let us study an example, the matrix $\begin{bmatrix} 1,2,3,0 \\ 2,4,6,0 \\ 5,0,6,3 \end{bmatrix}$ has a rank of 2, not 3, because there are only two hard vectors in it. The second row can be obtained by multiplying 2 to the top row.

Dr.C extends his idea: "When we solve coupled linear equations, the situation is similar to what we discuss here about vectors. Even if we have m equations for m unknowns, that situation does not guarantee that the problem has a unique solution. We need to check whether the given equations are all 'hard equations' or not. 'Soft equations' cannot be counted. If there are m unknowns in n *hard* equations, then the problem has unique solution if $m = n$; has infinite solutions if $m > n$; and has no solution if $m < n$."

Finally Dr.C says: "The word *soft* or *hard* used here is just an analogy, the real meaning is linearly dependent or linearly independent. Sometimes it is not clear that a vector or an equation is hard or soft, in that case we need to reduce the matrix to row reduced echelon form. Once that is done all equations or vectors left are hard."

13.3 "Mission impossible"

Some problems are really impossible to solve, like $2^x = -1$. Other times the questions may appear to be impossible, but actually are solvable. These questions may have hidden conditions. The process to solve an apparently impossible equation is an art in mathematics.

Today Dr.C discussed some questions with the students.

[100 chickens, 100 dollars]

"Five dollars can buy a hen, three dollars can buy a rooster. Three chicks together cost 1 dollar. Mrs. Smith used $100 and bought 100 of them. How many of each type did she buy?"

"This was a famous ancient problem," said Dr.C. He wrote two equations where x was the number of hens, y was the number of roosters and z was the number of chicks.

$$\begin{cases} x + y + z = 100 \\ 5x + 3y + \dfrac{1}{3}z = 100 \end{cases}$$

Felix said: "With only two equations how can we solve three unknowns? This question has infinite number of solutions. It is impossible to solve them definitely."

Margaret pointed out: "However, the number of hens, roosters and chicks can only be whole numbers between 0 and 100, isn't it?"

"Correct," said Dr.C. "That is the key to convert a mission impossible to a mission possible. The second equation is equivalent to

$15x + 9y + z = 300$, subtract the first equation from this one and simplify the result, we get $7x + 4y = 100$, therefore $y = 25 - \dfrac{7}{4}x$.

"Since y must be a whole number, the number of hens x must be a whole number between 0 and 14 and must be divided by 4. How many whole numbers between 0 and 14 can be divided by 4? Only four ($x = 0$, 4, 8, and 12). Once you know x, the value of y and z can be easily determined from the two equations. Thus we have four sets of answers, $(x, y, z) = (0, 25, 75)$, $(4, 18, 78)$, $(8, 11, 81)$ and $(12, 4, 84)$. If all three types are required (no zero) then there are three sets of answers."

[An equation that holds for any x value]

Next, Dr.C invited the students to solve the following problem: Find the two parameters a and b, such that the following equation holds for any value of x.

$$(2a - b - 11)x^2 - 3(a + 3b + 5)x - (19a - 6b - 94) = 0$$

Again, this looks like a "mission impossible". In one equation there are three unknowns a, b, and x. Plus, the equation must hold for all x values!

Dr.C smiled: "In order to satisfy the equation for *any x*, there is only one way: when the equation is $0x^2 + 0x + 0 = 0$. That is,

$$\begin{cases} 2a - b - 11 = 0 \\ a + 3b + 5 = 0 \end{cases}$$

"The answers are $a = 4$ and $b = -3$. Luckily now the value of $19a - 6b - 94$ is 0 too. When $a = 4$, $b = -3$ the original equation is

$0x^2 + 0x + 0 = 0$, it holds for any value of x. (The equation has no solution if the number 94 is changed to 93 or 95).

"Similarly, if two vectors $\vec{u}$ and $\vec{v}$ are not parallel, and if $(2m - 5n + 16)\vec{u} + (4m + 7n - 2)\vec{v} = 0$, then the only way to satisfy this equation for *any* non-parallel vectors $\vec{u}$ and $\vec{v}$ is that both parts must be zero at the same time:

$$\begin{cases} 2m - 5n + 16 = 0 \\ 4m + 7n - 2 = 0 \end{cases}$$

"The answers are $m = -3$ and $n = 2$."

13.4 "Overkill", apply higher math to basic geometry

Many math questions can be solved in different ways. Some methods are not simple, but they may provide different approaches with deeper meanings. Dr.C describes this phenomenon as "overkill", or "using anti-aircraft cannons to shoot a mosquito." The whole class laughs. Dr.C explains: "To a beginner of a math course we do not need to solve a simple, basic question by higher mathematics, but once you have learned more powerful math, why not try to apply them on some basic questions to see how it works?"

[Problem 1] Shapes of a figure

If we transform a geometric figure up, down, left or right several steps; or rotate it clockwise or counter clockwise; or fold it using either the x

or y axis as the symmetric axis to do reflection; we can do all of these on a grid paper point by point, step by step. Nevertheless we can also find the answers by higher mathematics using algebra or matrices.

Translating a point (a,b) k steps up, down, right or left, we get $(a,b+k)$, $(a,b-k)$, $(a-k,b)$, or $(a+k,b)$. This is the method of formula. A reflection in the x axis is expressed as a change from (a,b) to $(a,-b)$. A reflection in the y axis is expressed as a change from (a,b) to $(-a,b)$. A rotation $90°$, $180°$, or $270°$ clockwise changes the point (a,b) to $(b,-a)$, $(-a,-b)$, or $(-b,a)$ respectively.

Knowing the formula we can find the location of an image without the need of a diagram. If you want to do some kind of transformation to a triangle, just find the three new vertices by formula then connect the three new positions. All those formulas can be written in matrix form. For example a reflection using the x axis as the mirror can be expressed by the transformation matrix $\begin{bmatrix} 1 & 0 \\ 0 & -1 \end{bmatrix}$.

A rotation $90°$ counter clockwise about the origin can be expressed by the matrix $\begin{bmatrix} 0 & -1 \\ 1 & 0 \end{bmatrix}$, etc. Under this rotation the point $(-2,3)$ will move to the new position $(-3,-2)$.

$$\begin{bmatrix} 0 & -1 \\ 1 & 0 \end{bmatrix} \begin{bmatrix} -2 \\ 3 \end{bmatrix} = \begin{bmatrix} -3 \\ -2 \end{bmatrix}$$

This is the same as a rotation $270°$ clockwise about the origin.

[Problem 2] Geometric proof

The line segment connecting the midpoints of two sides of an arbitrary shape triangle is always parallel to the third side and is always equal to half of the length of the third side. In the diagram below M is the midpoint of the side AB, N is the midpoint of the side AC. Prove that $MN \parallel BC$ and $MN = \dfrac{1}{2} BC$.

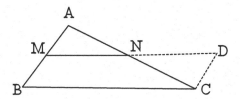

The way to prove the theorem in Euclidean geometry is to draw $CD \parallel BA$ and meet the extension of MN at point D. Then we try to prove that $\triangle AMN \cong \triangle CDN$, hence $MDCB$ is a parallelogram. This proof is strong in logic, simple and clear. Nothing beyond plane geometry is required.

Well, it can also be proved by vectors.

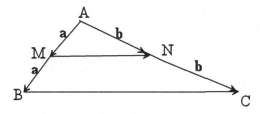

In the diagram vector $MN=AN - AM$, that is, $\vec{b} - \vec{a}$. Vector $BC=AC - AB$, that is, $2\vec{b} - 2\vec{a}$. Hence $BC=2MN$. This vector equality has the meaning on both the magnitudes (a ratio 2:1) and the direction (parallel).

237

Therefore we have proved both statements at one step. This is the fastest way to prove that theorem.

It can also be proved by algebra. Set up coordinates so that the origin is at point B and the x axis is along side BC. Assume that $AM=MB=a$ and $BC=2b$.

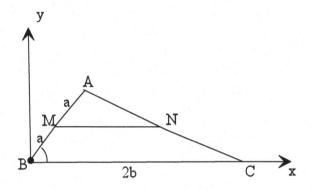

If we call the angle $\angle ABC$ as θ, then the three coordinates of the given triangle are $A(2a\cos\theta, 2a\sin\theta)$, $B(0,0)$, and $C(2b,0)$. There are three famous formulas in analytic geometry:

the midpoint $\left(\dfrac{x_1+x_2}{2}, \dfrac{y_1+y_2}{2}\right)$

the slope $m = \dfrac{y_2-y_1}{x_2-x_1}$

the distance between two points $d = \sqrt{(x_2-x_1)^2+(y_2-y_1)^2}$

From them we can find that the two midpoints are $M(a\cos\theta, a\sin\theta)$ and $N(a\cos\theta+b, a\sin\theta)$. The slope of MN is 0 and the length of it is b. Now we have proved that MN and BC are parallel (both have the same slope 0) and $MN = \dfrac{1}{2} BC$.

This method uses trigonometry and algebra. First write the coordinates of each point, the plane geometry question is changed into an analytic geometry question and we can use very powerful algebraic methods to solve an equation or coupled equations. This method is so powerful, that it becomes a very sharp weapon in combining the power of algebra and geometry.

Dr.C says: "The more difficult a geometry question is, the more powerful this algebra method is. Of course, to describe it as 'an overkill' or 'to use anti-aircraft cannons to shoot a mosquito', sounds scary. Why not just use more peaceful words to describe it as 'using a modern computer to do a basic question'?"

Chapter 14
Calculus - Differentiation

14.1 Understanding derivative rules

Senior grade students are learning calculus. Topics include derivative rules: the power rule, the product rule, the quotient rule and the chain rule.

In order to explain the chain rule, Dr.C drew two concentric circles and a function on the board: $f(x) = (2x^3 + 7x)^5$. Dr.C said: "I am going to explain the chain rule with this diagram. In this example the function has a two layer structure: the outer layer represents '5th power of something'; the inner circle represents the details of the inner structure $(2x^3 + 7x)$.

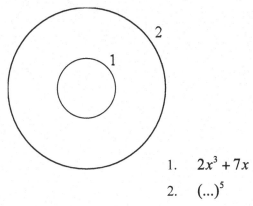

1. $2x^3 + 7x$
2. $(...)^5$

"When we calculate the derivative of a function we do the outer layer first. What is the derivative of x^5? it is $5x^4$. At this step we *ignore* the inside structures, view it simply as a 'solid monolithic bloc', ignoring all details in it, so that $(...)^5 \rightarrow 5(...)^4$. Next go to the inner layer, differentiate the inner structure $(2x^3 + 7x)$ and get $(6x^2 + 7)$ and multiply it to the result of the previous step and the problem is done.

"If there are three, four or more layers we still treat the problem in the same way. Starting from the outmost layer, do one layer at a time. When you do one layer ignore all details inside that layer, forget all finished layers. For example to find the derivative of $y = \sin \sqrt{x^3 - 2x - 1}$, study its structure first. It has three layers. First, the outside layer is a sine function whose derivative is a cosine function. The middle layer is a square root function whose derivative can be found with $\sqrt{} \rightarrow \dfrac{1}{2\sqrt{}}$. The inner layer $x^3 - 2x - 1$ has a derivative of $3x^2 - 2$. Multiply all these together we get

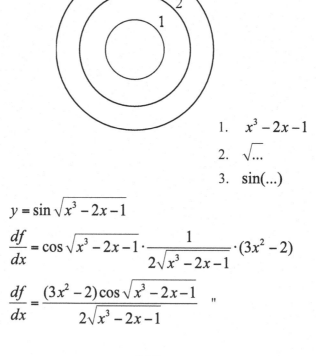

1. $x^3 - 2x - 1$
2. $\sqrt{...}$
3. $\sin(...)$

$$y = \sin \sqrt{x^3 - 2x - 1}$$

$$\frac{df}{dx} = \cos \sqrt{x^3 - 2x - 1} \cdot \frac{1}{2\sqrt{x^3 - 2x - 1}} \cdot (3x^2 - 2)$$

$$\frac{df}{dx} = \frac{(3x^2 - 2)\cos \sqrt{x^3 - 2x - 1}}{2\sqrt{x^3 - 2x - 1}} \quad "$$

242

Such a "layer by layer" method is simple and straight forward. The students like it. Together with the formula $\frac{dy}{dx} = \frac{dy}{du} \cdot \frac{du}{dv} \cdot \frac{dv}{dx}$, they understand the chain rule in more depth.

Dr.C continued: "The product rule and the quotient rule are easier. If you write the product rule as $\frac{d}{dx}(uv) = \frac{dv}{dx}u + \frac{du}{dx}v$, you are right. However, in the next step you learn the quotient rule, you may make a mistake and write the quotient rule as (*wrong*) $\frac{d}{dx}\left(\frac{u}{v}\right) = \frac{\frac{dv}{dx}u - \frac{du}{dx}v}{v^2}$. The correct formula is $\frac{d}{dx}\left(\frac{u}{v}\right) = \frac{\frac{du}{dx}v - \frac{dv}{dx}u}{v^2}$. Therefore we better write the product rule in the same order, that is $\frac{d}{dx}(uv) = \frac{du}{dx}v + \frac{dv}{dx}u$.

"We not only teach 'what is correct', but also tell you 'what is the most probable error'. In finding the derivatives, a common mistake is doing the two parts of a product at the same time, $\frac{d}{dx}(uv) = \frac{du}{dx}\frac{dv}{dx}$, $\frac{d}{dx}\left(\frac{u}{v}\right) = \frac{\frac{du}{dx}}{\frac{dv}{dx}}$ (both are *incorrect*). The most common error in applying the calculus differentiation chain rule is to do all layers in one step: like $\frac{d}{dx}(3x^2 + 7x)^5 = 5(6x + 7)^4$ (*incorrect*).

"Using our concentric circle concept, it is easier to avoid such mistakes."

14.2 A surprising talk about functions and derivatives

These days the students are learning how to calculate the derivatives of functions. They discuss the topic enthusiastically. Today Doug and Keel told Dr.C that they already knew how to evaluate derivatives of simple functions, but still needed to know more about the nature of derivatives.

Dr.C said: "Let us compare functions with their derivatives. First I must say: **For any given value of x, There is no relation between the value of $f(x)$ and $\dfrac{df}{dx}$.**"

Students were surprised. They doubted how that could be true.

"It is true," said Dr.C. "At any instant, there is no relation between $f(x)$ and $\dfrac{df}{dx}$. Using motion as an example, if $s(t)$ represents the position of an object at time t, then $\dfrac{ds}{dt}$ is its velocity. Only given the position at time t, it is impossible to know what its velocity at that instant is. The object may be at rest, may be moving forward or backward at any speed. The contrary is also true, if you know the velocity of an object at a time, you don't have enough information to decide its position at that time. Similar relationship exists between the velocity and the acceleration at the same time instant for a moving object. A billionaire has much more money than I, but if these days he is losing money and my little money is slowly increasing by 1 cent a day, then I can say to him with pride that 'as to the speed of increase in money, I am doing better than you'.

"How can we decide that a moving object is leaving the origin or approaching the origin? It is not just decided by the sign (positive or negative) of its velocity. Similarly, speeding up does not mean its acceleration must be positive, slowing down does not necessarily mean its acceleration is negative."

The students are surprised to know that if the speed is positive that does not necessarily mean the object is leaving the origin, or if the acceleration is positive that does not necessarily mean that the object is speeding up.

Dr.C said: "Assume that you are currently at the position $x = -10$ and have a positive velocity, you are moving towards origin from the left. If you are at the position $x = -10$ and have a negative velocity, you are moving away from the origin, moving toward a place even more negative."

Dr.C continued: "Let position, velocity and acceleration each be 0, solve the equation of $s(t) = 0$, $v(t) = 0$, and $a(t) = 0$. Figure out in what time span, each of them is positive or negative. If in a time period both s and v have the same sign (regardless of being both + or both −), the object is moving away from the origin. If they have opposite signs (regardless which is positive and which is negative) the object is moving towards the origin. Similarly if both v and a have the same sign the object is speeding up; if they have opposite signs the object is slowing down, regardless of which one (v or a) is positive or negative. The results are shown in the table below."

s	v	Description of motion
+	+	On the right of the origin, moving right, away from the origin
+	−	On the right of the origin, moving left, approaching the origin
−	+	On the left of the origin, moving right, approaching the origin
−	−	On the left of the origin, moving left, away from the origin

v	a	Description of motion
+	+	Moves right, accelerates right, speeding up
+	−	Moves right, accelerates left, slowing down
−	+	Moves left, accelerates right, slowing down
−	−	Moves left, accelerates left, speeding up

14.3 Comparison of derivatives and functions

Diane asked: "Dr.C, is the function itself more complicated, or the derivative of the same function more complicated?"

Dr.C said: "Good question. Is a function more complicated or simpler than its own derivative? I am glad to listen to you first. Let us have a discussion --- just remember to provide proper examples please."

George said: "If $f(x) = \dfrac{1}{2}x^2$, then $\dfrac{df}{dx} = x$, $\dfrac{d^2 f}{dx^2} = 1$, and

$\dfrac{d^3 f}{dx^3} = 0$. So I think the function is more complicated than its derivative. The more differentiation you do, the simpler the result becomes."

Helen said: "I do not agree. If $f(x) = \sqrt{x}$, then $\dfrac{df}{dx} = \dfrac{1}{2\sqrt{x}}$,

$\dfrac{d^2 f}{dx^2} = \dfrac{-1}{4\sqrt{x^3}}$.   The more you calculate, the more complicated it will be. So the function is simpler than its derivative."

Dr.C then drew three diagrams and said: "We cannot just see one point and forget the other. In the first diagram the function (shown as the solid curve) $y = (x^2 - 1)(x^2 - 4)$) is a 4th order polynomial, with one local maximum and two local minima. Its derivative (shown as the dashed curve) is a cubic function, with one maximum and one minimum. In this example the derivative is simpler than the original function.

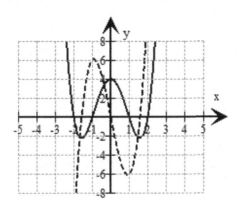

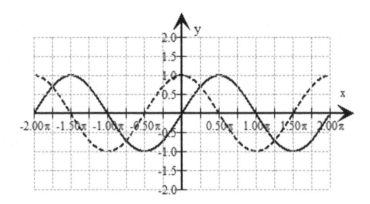

"In the second diagram the function (the solid curve $y = \sin x$) and its derivative (the dashed curve $y = \cos x$) are the same curve only shifted horizontally. The two have the same complexity.

"In the third diagram the function (the solid curve $y = \dfrac{x^2 - 1}{x^4 + 1}$) has two local maxima and one local minimum, its derivative (the dashed curve $\dfrac{dy}{dx} = \dfrac{-2x^5 + 4x^3 + 2x}{(x^4 + 1)^2}$) has two local maxima and 2 local minima and is more complicated than the original function. You may also compare the two expressions and agree that $\dfrac{dy}{dx}$ here is more complicated than y.

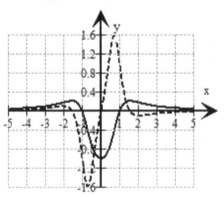

"Therefore simply to say which one is more complicated than the other is not scientific. We should analyze each individual situation, don't jump to conclusion.

"My friends, look outside the window. Snow melts, the ground starts to turn green, flowers are preparing to blossom. It is early spring! Let us sing a song to welcome the arriving of the most beautiful season of a year!"

14.4 Which quantity should not be used too early?

Dr.C's students have learned calculus for a month. They know how to find the derivative of a function; they are familiar with the rules of derivatives (the power rule, the product rule, the quotient rule, and the chain rule). Now they start to learn applications of derivatives, including related rates, optimal values, and curve sketching.

Different quantities are related to each other. For example perimeter, area and volume are related to the length of sides. A change of one causes a change to another. Dr.C says: "Some given quantities should not be used too early, some should never be used at all in calculating related rates questions."

"Feel too abstract? Let us study some examples. The side length of a square increases at the rate 1.5 m/s. What is the rate of the increase of its area when the side reaches 4 m?

"Such a problem is easy. Starting from the area formula, differentiates both sides with respect to time t:

$$A = x^2$$

$$\frac{dA}{dt} = 2x\frac{dx}{dt} = 2(4)(1.5) = 12m^2/s$$

"In this question the given quantity 4 m should not be used too early. If you input $x = 4\,m$ before you calculate the derivative, the area would become a constant (16 m^2) and its derivative would be 0. We should always start with a changing status, not a static view, then find its time derivative. Input that 4 m only at the end of the calculation.

"In some questions a given quantity may even be useless, it should not be used in your calculation at all. For instance, if the length of a water trough is L and its cross section is an equilateral triangle of altitude H, when water is poured in at a given rate R, find the speed of the increase of water level in the trough when the water level is h.

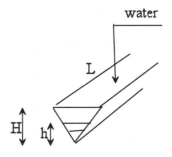

"In this question the height H is useless. Never put it into your calculation. Why not? Because when water is poured in, the level of water increases gradually. Before the level reaches the highest possible limit, that limit height is useless. Water level increasing rate is independent of the highest top level. In this question the rate of water level increasing is determined by the water input rate, the shape of the cross-section (an equilateral triangle), the instant (when water level is h), but not the maximum height H.

"Another question is the rate of change of the shadow length, posted by a lamp on a street. For example a lamppost is $a = 5$ m high, there is a lamp on the top of the post. A person (height b = 2 m) is walking away from the post with a speed v = 1.5 m/s. When she is y = 7 m from the post, what is the rate of change of her shadow length x with respect to time?

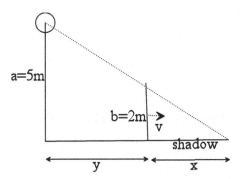

"From the knowledge of similar triangles we know $\dfrac{a}{b} = \dfrac{x+y}{x}$,

hence $x = \dfrac{b}{a-b} y$ and $\dfrac{dx}{dt} = \left(\dfrac{b}{a-b}\right)\dfrac{dy}{dt}$. In order to find the rate of

increase of the shadow $\dfrac{dx}{dt}$, we only need the information that $a = 5m$,

$b = 2m$, $\dfrac{dy}{dt} = 1.5m/s$. We do not need to know where that person is at a

particular time. The 7 m given in the problem is completely useless; the answer would be the same if we change that 7 m to 4 m or 13 m.

"In this question x and y satisfy a linear relation, $\dfrac{dx}{dt}$ is only related

to $\dfrac{dy}{dt}$, not to y. Whereas in the square area question, the area A and the side

length x are not linearly related to each other. The area $A = x^2$, so that

$\dfrac{dA}{dt} = 2x \dfrac{dx}{dt}$. Do you see? The rate $\dfrac{dA}{dt}$ is not only determined by $\dfrac{dx}{dt}$, but also by x. Since the relation is not linear and the answer $\dfrac{dA}{dt}$ depends on both $\dfrac{dx}{dt}$ and x, the side length x should also be considered --- just remember not to input it too early."

14.5 Tips to do implicit differentiation

Tom asked Dr.C: "Can you give us any tip on implicit differentiation?"

Dr.C answered: "Certainly. Tips live everywhere, waiting for us to discover. First, let me ask you why do we want to learn implicit differentiation? Now that $x^2 - y = 0$ is the same as $y = x^2$, why not just use $y = x^2$ to find its derivative explicitly?"

Tom replied: "If the function is complicated, it won't be possible to be written in explicit form. For example it is hard to re-write $e^{3x^2} \sin(2y) - \ln x \ln y = 1$ into an explicit form $y = f(x)$, so we still need to learn the implicit way."

"Excellent!" said Dr.C. "Sometimes we can change an implicit formula into an explicit formula but it is faster if we do not change it. If we want to find the derivative $\dfrac{dy}{dx}$ of $(x^2 + y^2)^2 = 4x^2 y$ at point (1, 1), we may calculate the derivative implicitly and get :

$$2(x^2 + y^2)(2x + 2y\tfrac{dy}{dx}) = 8xy + 4x^2\tfrac{dy}{dx}$$

Then instead of solving for $\dfrac{dy}{dx}$, we better directly substitute $x = 1$ and

$y = 1$ to get $2(1+1)(2+2\tfrac{dy}{dx}) = 8 + 4\tfrac{dy}{dx}$, hence $\dfrac{dy}{dx} = 0$.

"Next, let us study $x^{-2}y^6 + 2y^{-2} - 6 = 0$. We do not like negative exponents; therefore we multiply both sides by x^2y^2 first, change it to $y^8 + 2x^2 - 6x^2y^2 = 0$ and then find its derivative by implicit differentiation.

"Sometimes we can use the given relation to simplify the result. In order to differentiate $x^2 - 3xy + y^2 = 10$ to find its second order derivative $\dfrac{d^2y}{dx^2}$, we do it the implicit way and find $2x - 3y - 3x\tfrac{dy}{dx} + 2y\tfrac{dy}{dx} = 0$, so that $\dfrac{dy}{dx} = \dfrac{3y - 2x}{2y - 3x}$. The second derivative can be obtained by the quotient rule, $\dfrac{d^2y}{dx^2} = \dfrac{10x^2 - 30xy + 10y^2}{(2y - 3x)^3}$.

"At this time don't forget to use the original equation $x^2 - 3xy + y^2 = 10$ to simplify the numerator of the answer. The final result is quite simple, $\dfrac{d^2y}{dx^2} = \dfrac{100}{(2y - 3x)^3}$."

14.6 Optimal value problems, converting hard to easy

Katie and Peter discussed minimum and maximum problems in calculus. Katie told Peter: "If we see two unknowns we may change them into one unknown first, then find its derivative, let the derivative equal to zero and solve for x."

Peter said: "Oh, yes. If we want to design a cylinder of volume $500cm^3$ using minimum material for its surface, we face two things, volume and surface area. The given volume is a constraint $V = \pi r^2 h = 500cm^3$, using this constrain we can change two unknowns r and h into one unknown in the formula of the surface area. After that differentiate it and let the derivative be zero to find the optimal values of r and h, then find the surface area."

Dr.C joined their discussion and pointed out: "Be aware, A zero derivative is only one possible path to reach the optimum. A zero derivative may not lead to a maximum or a minimum (as $x = 0$ for $y = x^3$). Also not every optimal value comes out at a place where the derivative is zero (a minimum or maximum can be the point where the function exists but the derivative does not exist, as $y = |x|$ at x = 0; or an end point like $\sqrt{x}$ at $x = 0$).

Dr.C added: "In practice there are some useful tips to help us convert a harder problem into an easier question."

[Example 1]   Find the maximum area of the rectangle in the diagram, the radius of the circle is 10 cm.

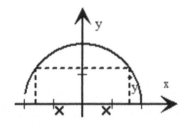

"The equation of the upper semi-circle is $y = \sqrt{100 - x^2}$. The area of the rectangle is $A = 2xy = 2x\sqrt{100 - x^2}$. It is not simple to evaluate the derivative directly from this formula and let $\dfrac{dA}{dx} = 0$. The tip here is to square both sides first, so that we have $A^2 = 4x^2(100 - x^2) = 400x^2 - 4x^4$, then find its derivative (which is easy). Another tip is to call the base of the rectangle as $2x$ instead of x to avoid fractions."

[**Example 2**] A person starts from point P in the diagram to go to point F. The width of the river is 300 m and QF = 800 m. Her speed of rowing in water is 2 m/s and walking on the land is 3 m/s. Where is the best location (R) for her to land, such that the total time is the minimum?

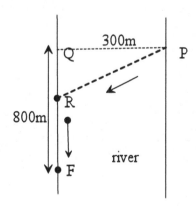

"Some textbooks define RF= x so PR= $\sqrt{(800-x)^2 + 300^2}$ and the total time is $t = \dfrac{x}{3} + \dfrac{\sqrt{(800-x)^2 + 300^2}}{2}$, then calculate the derivative $\dfrac{dt}{dx}$.

"Our method is simpler. We define QR as x so the total time is

$$t = \frac{800-x}{3} + \frac{\sqrt{x^2 + 300^2}}{2},$$

"Then evaluate the derivative from there. As you can see, we simplified the most difficult part (the part inside the square root sign)."

[**Example 3**] At 1 pm car A is 160 km south of car B. Car A goes north with a speed 60 km/h, car B goes west with a speed 80 km/h. What is the shortest distance L between them?

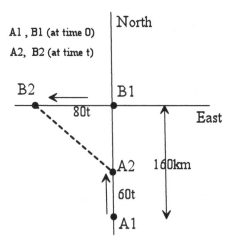

"The normal way is to apply the Pythagorean theorem and use implicit differentiation. Instead, we may also use explicit differentiation. Assume that the time is t, then the distance A1 --- A2 is $60t$ and B1 --- B2 is $80t$.

$$L^2 = (160 - 60t)^2 + (80t)^2$$

"Then evaluate the derivative with respect to time t on both sides. Remember that it is easier to use L^2, instead of $L = \sqrt{(160 - 60t)^2 + (80t)^2}$ to find the time. When L^2 is an optimal value, so is L.

[Example 4] "The 'fence law' introduced in Section 9.2 is still correct in calculus. Using our method we know the answer *before* we start to do the question."

Katie and Peter made notes. After the lesson they tried many creative methods to evaluate the optimal values in calculus.

14.7 Three ways to decide the signs in curve sketching

Curve sketching is an important part of calculus. To get a correct graph we need to understand the behavior of the curve thoroughly: In which region does the curve increase (decrease)? Where are the locations of the local and absolute minima and maxima? In which region does the curve concave up (concave down)? To know these we need to decide the signs of the derivatives $\dfrac{df}{dx}$ and $\dfrac{d^2 f}{dx^2}$.

Dr.C watched his students doing curve sketching and discovered that they used different ways to decide the positive or negative sign of the derivative. Therefore he invited the students to explain their methods. Using derivative $\dfrac{df}{dx} = (x+3)(x-1)(x-2)(x-5)$ as an example, this derivative has 4 zeroes: $x = -3$, 1, 2, 5. These four zeroes divide the x axis into five regions, as shown in the following diagram (not drawn to scale).

Cheryl said first: "I try find a test point in each section, check the sign of the four factors to know the sign of the overall derivative function. For instance to know the region $2 < x < 5$ I tried $x = 4$. At $x = 4$ the signs of the four factors are: $(4+3)$ positive, $(4-1)$ positive, $(4-2)$ positive, $(4-5)$ negative. Therefore $\dfrac{df}{dx}$ is negative."

Harry said: "My method is similar to Cheryl's, but a little bit simpler. I do not substitute test values to see whether a factor is negative or positive. Instead, I consider $(x-a)$. The expression $(x-a)$ is negative when x is left of a, and it is positive when x is right of a. For example $(x-1)$ uses $x = 1$ as a dividing point, $(x-1)$ is negative left of the separation and is positive right of the separation. Similarly $(x+3) = (x-(-3))$ uses -3 as the dividing point, it is negative for $x < -3$ and positive in all regions where $x > -3$. So I got the following results without inputting any test value."

x		-3	1	2	5	
$(x+3)$	$-$	$+$	$+$	$+$	$+$	
$(x-1)$	$-$	$-$	$+$	$+$	$+$	
$(x-2)$	$-$	$-$	$-$	$+$	$+$	
$(x-5)$	$-$	$-$	$-$	$-$	$+$	
$\dfrac{df}{dx}$	$+$	$-$	$+$	$-$	$+$	

"That is fast," said Pam. "Let me tell you my way. Since $\dfrac{df}{dx} = (x+3)(x-1)(x-2)(x-5)$ is a fourth order polynomial of x, its graph has a W shape (or a M shape if the leading coefficient is negative). Consider the four zeroes and a W shape, a simplified graph looks like this:

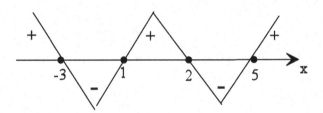

"Thus we know the + (above the x axis) and − (below the x axis) regions. Once we know these we know in which region the function is increasing or decreasing."

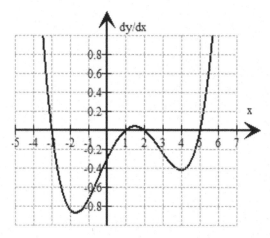

Graph of $\dfrac{df}{dx} = (x+3)(x-1)(x-2)(x-5)$

Jessica said: " My way is to discuss the signs of $\dfrac{df}{dx}$ and $\dfrac{d^2 f}{dx^2}$ together. My example is $f(x) = x^3 + 3x^2 - 9x - 2$. This function has $\dfrac{df}{dx} = 3x^2 + 6x - 9 = 3(x+3)(x-1)$ and $\dfrac{d^2 f}{dx^2} = 6x + 6 = 6(x+1)$.

"If $\dfrac{df}{dx} = 0$, we have $x = -3$ and $x = 1$. If $\dfrac{d^2 f}{dx^2} = 0$, we have $x = -1$. Consider $x = -3$, $x = 1$, and $x = -1$ at the same time, we get the following results (CD = concave down, CU = concave up):

x		-3		-1		1	
$(x+3)$	$-$		$+$		$+$		$+$
$(x-1)$	$-$		$-$		$-$		$+$
$(x+1)$	$-$		$-$		$+$		$+$
$\dfrac{df}{dx}$	$+$		$-$		$-$		$+$
$\dfrac{d^2 f}{dx^2}$	$-$		$-$		$+$		$+$
$f(x)$	CD		CD		CU		CU
	inc		dec		dec		inc

"With the information here (increasing, decreasing, concave up, concave down) plus some special points (optimal values, x and y intercepts) we can sketch the graph of $f(x)$ now."

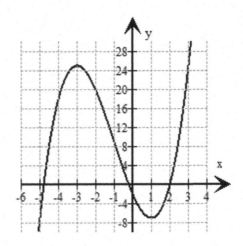

Chapter 15
Calculus - Integration

15.1 Integral by parts, which is *u*? which is *v*?

Today's calculus lesson was active. Kevin asked Dr.C: "We know integral by parts is useful, some integrals can only be done by that method. However, when we apply the formula $\int u\,dv = uv - \int v\,du$, which part is u and which part is v?"

Dr.C smiled, answered: "Let me tell you a method which is not found in textbooks. I call the functions x, x^2, x^3 ... as 'soft functions'. Such soft functions cannot live long when you calculate their derivatives again and again. The derivative of x^n is nx^{n-1}, the next derivative is $n(n-1)x^{n-2}$, the next, next derivative is $n(n-1)(n-2)x^{n-3}$, and so on. Continue this way it will become a constant at some point, and after that all derivatives will be 0 so we successfully 'kill' that function. If I can 'kill' a function by differentiation I call it a 'soft function'.

"On the other hand, the derivatives of e^x is always e^x, the derivative of $\sin x$ is $\cos x$, continue to differentiate you get $-\sin x$, $-\cos x$, then back to $\sin x$. You cannot 'kill' e^x, $\sin x$ or $\cos x$. Such a function is stubborn that you cannot 'kill' it by finding its derivatives. I call it a 'hard function', meaning that it is hard to be eliminated by differentiation.

"When you apply integral by parts if the integrand has two parts, one soft part and one hard part, usually we define the **soft part as *u* and the**

hard part as v. For example $\int x^2 \cos x\,dx$, let $u = x^2$, $dv = \cos x\,dx$ (i.e., let $v = \sin x$). Apply integral by parts twice then x^2 disappears. The further you go the simpler it becomes. When u is 'killed', the outcome is clear. If you define $\cos x$ as u, then the power of x will increase, the problem becomes more and more difficult."

Students welcomed this "not found in textbook" rule. Dr.C added: "Although this rule of thumb is good, applicable to many questions, I still need to supplement three notes. Notes No.1, if both parts are 'hard', then you may consider either one as u, and do it by parts twice. This method is found in textbooks. For example the integral $\int e^x \sin x\,dx$ yields an answer of $\frac{1}{2}e^x(\sin x - \cos x) + C$ whether you consider $\sin x$ as u or consider e^x as u.

"Notes No.2, if you see $\ln x$ or $\tan^{-1} x$, define it as u. For instance to evaluate $\int x \ln x\,dx$ or $\int x \tan^{-1} x\,dx$, let u be $\ln x$ or $\tan^{-1} x$.

"Notes No.3, when you apply the above rule, be flexible. To solve more complicated problems you may need a better idea. For instance $\int \frac{xe^x}{(x+1)^2}\,dx$, defining e^x as u or x as u makes integration difficult. A better way is to define $u = xe^x$ (hence $du = (1+x)e^x dx$), and define $dv = \frac{1}{(x+1)^2}\,dx$ so that $v = -\frac{1}{(x+1)}$. Apply integral by parts:

$$\int u\,dv = uv - \int v\,du = -\frac{xe^x}{(x+1)} + \int \frac{1}{(x+1)}(1+x)e^x\,dx$$

$$= -\frac{xe^x}{x+1} + e^x + C = \frac{e^x}{x+1} + C$$

Kevin asked a different question: "In substitution, how do we define u?"

Dr.C said: "Well, let me tell you another 'rule of thumb', which you will not find in any textbook. My tip is: *whichever part you don't like, define it as u.* Therefore, which part gives you trouble, define it as u in substitution, then check whether the rest can be related to du. If you want to do $\int x^7 \sqrt{5+3x^8} dx$, which part do you hate? Of course you would like the simple x^7. Let $u = 5 + 3x^8$, then $x^7 dx$ is $\frac{1}{24} du$. Apply substitution we get $\int x^7 \sqrt{5+3x^8} dx = \frac{1}{24} \int \sqrt{u} du$, the answer is $\frac{1}{36}(5+3x^8)^{\frac{3}{2}} + C$.

"The more you think about when you practise, the better you can do integration problems," concluded Dr.C.

15.2 Partial fraction integration – new method

Dr.C's student Victor today challenged Dr.C: "Can you do partial fraction integration without long division?"

When we use partial fraction method to evaluate an integral, the first step is to check the integrand. Does the numerator have a lower exponent than the denominator? If yes, then no problem, you may start partial fraction. For example $\int \frac{2x}{x^2-1} dx$, we can directly factor the denominator into two parts. Such a process can be found in any textbook ($\int \frac{2x}{x^2-1} dx = \int \frac{A}{x-1} dx + \int \frac{B}{x+1} dx$).

In case the numerator has a power higher than or equal to that of the denominator, we need to reduce the power on the top first. To do so the textbook method is to apply long division. For example $\int \dfrac{x^3 - 5x^2 + x}{x^2 - x - 2} dx$, the numerator ($x^3$) has a power higher than the denominator (x^2). We need to do a long division first. $(x^3 - 5x^2 + x) \div (x^2 - x - 2) = (x - 4)$, with remainder $(-x - 8)$.

So that we have:

$$\frac{x^3 - 5x^2 + x}{x^2 - x - 2} = (x - 4) - \frac{x + 8}{x^2 - x - 2} = (x - 4) + \frac{A}{x - 2} + \frac{B}{x + 1},$$

Then calculate the two coefficients A and B. This is the normal way.

Today Victor challenged Dr.C to use another approach instead of the long division to do partial fraction.

Dr.C praised Victor first, encouraged all students to challenge the teacher. Then he answered: "Without division we can also add one term and subtract the same term from the numerator, create a part same as the denominator, then simplify the rational expression. For example:

$$\int \frac{x^2}{x^2 - 1} dx = \int \frac{x^2 - 1 + 1}{x^2 - 1} dx$$

$$= \int 1 + \frac{1}{x^2 - 1} dx = x + \int \frac{1}{(x - 1)(x + 1)} dx$$

(Add 1 subtract 1, create a part same as the denominator then cancel. After that, do partial fractions.)

266

"For the problem $\int \frac{x^3 - 5x^2 + x}{x^2 - x - 2} dx$, we do the same. Write x^3 as $x(x^2 - x - 2)$, the extra part is $-x^2 - 2x$. The next term $-5x^2$ then becomes $-4(x^2 ...)$, etc.

$$\int \frac{x^3 - 5x^2 + x}{x^2 - x - 2} dx = \int \frac{x(x^2 - x - 2) - 4(x^2 - x - 2) - (x + 8)}{x^2 - x - 2} dx$$

$$= \int x dx - 4 \int 1 dx - \int \frac{x + 8}{(x - 2)(x + 1)} dx$$

"The denominator of the last part can be factored. The problem then becomes a usual partial fraction integral problem.

$$\int \frac{x + 8}{(x - 2)(x + 1)} dx = A \int \frac{1}{x - 2} dx + B \int \frac{1}{x + 1} dx$$

"Compare the two sides:

$$\frac{x + 8}{(x - 2)(x + 1)} = \frac{A}{x - 2} + \frac{B}{x + 1} = \frac{A(x + 1) + B(x - 2)}{(x - 2)(x + 1)}$$

"Since the denominators are the same, we only need to check the numerators:

$$x + 8 = A(x + 1) + B(x - 2) = (A + B)x + (A - 2B)$$

"Now we can either solve the coupled equations $\begin{cases} A + B = 1 \\ A - 2B = 8 \end{cases}$, or let

$x = 2$ to find A and let $x = -1$ to find B. The answers are $A = \dfrac{10}{3}$ and

$B = -\dfrac{7}{3}$. The rest is easy."

Finally Dr.C said: "This method may not be simpler than long division, but it does provide an alternative way to prepare the function for partial fraction integration. Even if the problem does not belong to the partial fraction type, we can still apply the method to complete an integral. For example

$$\int \frac{x^2}{x^2+1}\,dx = \int \frac{x^2+1-1}{x^2+1}\,dx = \int 1\,dx - \int \frac{1}{x^2+1}\,dx = x - \arctan x + C$$

"'There is more than one way to skin a cat', a smart rabbit built three caves to hide herself," said Dr.C. 'The more ways you master, the more flexible you can treat a problem. If one way seems to be hard, you still have other ways to try. So, why not learn an alternative method?"

15.3 The washer method and the shell method

The students wanted to discuss volume integration. Tony asked: "This part is complicated. Can you explain the various formulas for us?"

Dr.C said: "Yes. The given function may be in the form of $y = f(x)$ or $x = g(y)$; the rotational axis may be the x-axis or the y-axis. So we have four combinations:

Case 1: $y = f(x)$ rotates about the x axis. $V = \pi \int_a^b |f(x)|^2 \, dx$.

Case 2: $x = g(y)$ rotates about the y axis. $V = \pi \int_c^d |g(y)|^2 \, dy$.

Case 2 is similar to case 1, only with x and y switched.

Case 3: $y = f(x)$ rotates about the y axis. $V = 2\pi \int_a^b xf(x)dx$.

Case 4: $x = g(y)$ rotates about the x axis. $V = 2\pi \int_c^d yg(y)dy$.

Case 4 is similar to case 3, only with x and y switched.

"Case 1 and case 2 apply the washer method. Case 3 and case 4 apply the cylindrical shell method.

"In a simple problem $y = f(x)$ can be changed to $x = g(y)$ form. For example the function $y = 3x - 1$ is identical to $x = \dfrac{y+1}{3}$, therefore case 1 and case 4 are both applicable. You may change a '$x = g(y)$ rotating about the x axis' question into a '$y = f(x)$ rotating about the x-axis' question, so formulas for case 4 and case 1 can be linked together in a simple problem. Similarly case 3 and case 2 can also be linked together.

"However, in more complex problems it is impossible to convert $x = g(y)$ into $y = f(x)$, in those problems only one formula can be applied.

"Be careful when you do such an exchange. To see this, please calculate the volume obtained by rotating the area bounded by $y = x^2$, $x = 0$, $x = 2$ about the y axis."

Hill did the calculation and said: "When $0 \le x \le 2$, $y = x^2$ is the same as $x = \sqrt{y}$, therefore when such a curve rotates about the y axis we can either view it as a type 3 question ($V = 2\pi \int_0^2 x(x^2)dx = 8\pi$), or a type 2 question ($V = \pi \int_0^4 (\sqrt{y})^2 dy = 8\pi$). Am I right?"

Dr.C said: "I am sorry, you are not right."

Why not? Hill and Tony looked suspicious. Both methods gave the same result 8π. Why did Dr.C say that?

Dr.C drew the following diagram and explained: "When you consider it as a case 2 problem, the washer method $V = \pi \int_0^4 (\sqrt{y})^2 dy$ evaluates the volume of the solid B in the diagram. On the other hand a case 3 (the shell method) formula calculates the rotational volume of part A. These two volumes (A and B) **happen to be equal** to each other. Only the method of case 3 (the shell method) gives the correct answer for part A."

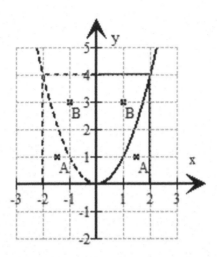

"We should also study the link between the two methods. If we combine part A with part B, we get a right cylinder of height 4 and radius 2. The volume of such a cylinder is $V = \pi r^2 h = \pi(2)^2(4) = 16\pi$. Hence when A is 8π, part B is $16\pi - 8\pi = 8\pi$ too. They *happen to be* the same in number but actually with different meanings. We can use type 2 formula instead of type 3 formula to evaluate the volume obtained by rotating the area bounded by $y = x^2$, $x = 0$, $x = 2$ about the y axis. However **the correct way must include a subtraction**: The cylinder volume minus type 2 answer ($16\pi - 8\pi = 8\pi$) equals the correct answer --- the volume found from type 3 formula."

Tony and Hill understood the important difference between the shell method and the washer method, as well as the link between these two methods.

15.4 Rotate an area about a line parallel to an axis

Jimmy asked Dr.C: "We learned how to find the rotational volume when an area rotates about the x-axis or the y-axis. If the rotational axis is a line parallel to, but not the same as a coordinate axis, what can we do? The method taught in school is hard."

Dr.C answered: "In your textbook you can of course find a method, but if you want to know more, I can show you my way. *'All roads lead to Rome'*. Besides the method in your textbook, we can find a different approach to solve the same problem. My way is **'to change a non-standard problem to a standard problem'**. "

"For example, an area enclosed by $y = x - 3$, $y = 0$ and $x = 4$, rotates about the straight line $x = 2$, find the rotational volume."

"It is not hard to see that the enclosed area is a triangle with vertices $(3,0)$, $(4,0)$, and $(4,1)$. My method is to **shift the coordinate axis**, change a non-standard (x,y) question into a standard (u,v) question. Here u is the new x, and v is the new y. Let us use the rotational axis $x = 2$ as the new v axis, use the point $(2,0)$ as the new origin, set up the new u axis. The new coordinate system is parallel to the old one.

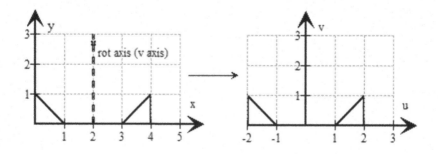

"A comparison between the old and the new coordinate systems leads to the following relations: $y = v$, and $x = u + 2$. Using these relations we can re-write the given x, y boundaries in the new u, v coordinate system. For example the old boundary $y = x - 3$ now becomes $v = (u + 2) - 3$, which is the same as $v = u - 1$ (or $u = v + 1$). In the new coordinate system the problem becomes standard --- an area enclosed by $u = v + 1$, $v = 0$, $u = 2$ **rotates about the new v axis.**

"Since it is now standard (rotating about a coordinate axis), we can directly apply the formula to evaluate the rotational volume.

"We can consider it as a case 3 problem (see the previous section) and apply the cylindrical shell method, so that

$$V = 2\pi \int_1^2 u f(u) du = 2\pi \int_1^2 u(u - 1) du = \frac{5\pi}{3}.$$

"Equivalently we can also consider it as a case 2 problem (be careful, as we said in the previous section). Use the cylinder volume (height 1, radius 2, $V_1 = \pi r^2 h = \pi (2)^2 (1) = 4\pi$; or $V_1 = \pi \int_0^1 2^2 dv$), subtract the inner part volume $V_2 = \pi \int_0^1 |g(v)|^2 dv = \pi \int_0^1 (v + 1)^2 dv$. Together we can write it as

$$V = \pi \int_0^1 (2^2 - (v + 1)^2) dv = \frac{5\pi}{3}$$ (the same answer).

"We use a coordinate translation; change a non-standard problem (rotating about a line other than the axis) to a standard problem (rotating about a coordinate axis). For such a standard question we have ready formulas to apply."

273

15.5 Is there a simple way to evaluate improper integrals?

March break is coming. Dr.C's students are anxiously preparing to go abroad to enjoy the week-long vacation. Some plan to fly to Europe to see the Mediterranean; some want to visit Australia or Asia; some students want to cruise the Atlantic Ocean or travel to the Caribbean islands; some of them plan to visit Africa, including a tour to see the Great Pyramids.

Time flies! The study time before March Break is valuable. The students surround Dr.C and ask: "Is there a simple way to evaluate improper integrals?"

Amy says: "Improper integrals are hard and complicated. They give me a head ache. Do we have to write them as limits every time?"

Dr.C replies: "Well, there is a short cut, but be very careful when you use it. Pay attention to the conditions under which it can be applied. The method is ignoring the integral limits first, treat the integral temporarily as if it were an ordinary indefinite integral and solve it. Once this is done, substitute the upper and the lower limits.

"For example, to evaluate $\int_0^\infty \frac{1}{x^2+1} dx$, we calculate $\int \frac{1}{x^2+1} dx$ first. The answer is $\tan^{-1} x$ (plus C). Come back to our question:

$$\int_0^\infty \frac{1}{x^2+1} dx = \tan^{-1} \infty - \tan^{-1} 0 = \frac{\pi}{2} - 0 = \frac{\pi}{2}.$$

This way is simple and the answer obtained is correct. Here is another example, $\int_0^9 \frac{1}{\sqrt{x}}\,dx$ is an improper integral. We do

$\int \frac{1}{\sqrt{x}}\,dx = 2\sqrt{x} + C$ first, substitute 9 and 0 we get the answer 6. This answer is also correct.

"Please remember the following points:

"[1]   When you write ' $\tan^{-1}\infty$ ' , you mean $\lim_{A\to\infty}\tan^{-1}A$. Similarly if you get e^∞, it is ∞; if you get $e^{-\infty}$, it is $\frac{1}{e^\infty} = 0$, in both cases it is defined and understood *as limits*.

"[2] This short cut is not strict, only something to be used informally (for example on a piece of scratch paper). For instance the correct and strict way to write the integral $\int_{-1}^{1} \frac{1}{(x+1)^{\frac{2}{3}}}\,dx$ is:

$$\int_{-1}^{1} \frac{1}{(x+1)^{\frac{2}{3}}}\,dx = \lim_{\varepsilon\to-1^+}\int_{\varepsilon}^{1} \frac{1}{(x+1)^{\frac{2}{3}}}\,dx$$
$$= 3\sqrt[3]{2} - \lim_{\varepsilon\to-1^+} 3\sqrt[3]{1+\varepsilon} = 3\sqrt[3]{2} - 0 = 3\sqrt[3]{2}$$

If we evaluate the indefinite integral first, we get $\int \frac{1}{(x+1)^{\frac{2}{3}}}\,dx = 3\sqrt[3]{x+1}$. Now substitute 1 and −1, we have the correct answer $3\sqrt[3]{2}$. This short cut method is indeed fast and easy but not strict. It is only recommended for solving multiple choice questions where only the answer (not the process) is important.

275

"[3] If there is an interruption (a discontinuous point) on the path between the two ends of an integral, we **cannot apply** this method. For instance it is **wrong** to evaluate the integral $\int_0^5 \frac{1}{x-1} dx$ as

$\ln|x-1|\big|_{x=0}^{x=5} = \ln 4 - \ln 1 = \ln 4$, since $\int_0^5 \frac{1}{x-1} dx = \int_0^1 \frac{1}{x-1} dx + \int_1^5 \frac{1}{x-1} dx$ and both integrals do not exist.

"[4] If the improper integral is from negative infinity to positive infinity this short cut method should not be used. We know that $\int_{-n}^{n} x\, dx = 0$ is correct for any finite n, but $\int_{-\infty}^{\infty} x\, dx$ is undefined.

$$\int_{-\infty}^{\infty} x\,dx = \int_{-\infty}^{0} x\,dx + \int_{0}^{\infty} x\,dx = \lim_{A\to-\infty} \int_{A}^{0} x\,dx + \lim_{B\to\infty} \int_{0}^{B} x\,dx$$

$$= (0 - \tfrac{1}{2}\lim_{A\to\infty} A^2) + (\tfrac{1}{2}\lim_{B\to\infty} B^2 - 0)$$

"The two integrals are not related. The speed and the manner for each of them to approach infinity is independent, therefore the two parts do not cancel each other.

"Here is a summary: An integral from minus infinity to infinity cannot apply this method. If there is a discontinuous point between the two ends of an integral, we cannot apply this method (cannot cancel, cannot interrupt). Other than these, improper integrals can be treated as if they were ordinary indefinite integrals then substitute the upper limit and the lower limit. *This short cut, if it can be used, should be used on scratch paper only.* It is informal. It does simplify and speed up your calculation when you answer multiple choice type integration questions."

15.6 Linear differential equations

Here in this quiet small North American town, Dr.C's students are back from their spring break vacations. Dr.C first welcomed the students back from wonderful trips around the world.

Today's class is about linear differential equations. The method in textbooks is to introduce an integral factor and apply the formula $y = e^{-\int p dx} \int q(x) e^{\int p dx} dx$ to find the solution of a linear differential equation $\dfrac{dy}{dx} + p(x)y = q(x)$.

Dr.C says: "In order to understand this topic thoroughly, let me tell you one more method."

[Method 1] Convert integral constant C into variable C(x)

Example: $\dfrac{dy}{dx} - \dfrac{2}{x}y = x^2$. Step 1 is to forget the right side and solve the homogeneous equation $\dfrac{dy}{dx} - \dfrac{2}{x}y = 0$. Once the right side is omitted the equation suddenly becomes variable separable. That is, $\dfrac{dy}{dx} = \dfrac{2y}{x}$ or $\dfrac{dy}{y} = 2\dfrac{dx}{x}$. Integrate both sides and we get the general solution $y = Cx^2$, where C is an arbitrary constant produced by the integration. Note that this $y = Cx^2$ is not the solution of the original linear differential equation, but only the solution of the simplified, homogeneous equation.

How can we find the solution of the original linear differential equation? Treat the constant C as $C(x)$, a function of x, then $y = Cx^2$ becomes $y = C(x)x^2$. Its derivative is $\dfrac{dy}{dx} = \dfrac{dC}{dx}x^2 + 2Cx$. Substitute both $y = Cx^2$ and $\dfrac{dy}{dx}$ back to the original equation $\dfrac{dy}{dx} - \dfrac{2}{x}y = x^2$, we see a spectacular phenomenon: the two terms of C suddenly cancel each other and disappear simultaneously!

The equation $\dfrac{dC}{dx}x^2 + 2Cx \quad -\dfrac{2}{x}(Cx^2) = x^2$ is changed to $\dfrac{dC}{dx}x^2 = x^2$, that is $\dfrac{dC}{dx} = 1$.

Dr. C says: "Remember, the cancellation of the C terms is inevitable. If you still see a term with $C(x)$ after this step, something is already wrong. After the cancellation the equation only contains $\dfrac{dC}{dx}$, no $C(x)$. In this question $\dfrac{dC}{dx} = 1$ so $C = x + k$ where k is an arbitrary constant. The solution of the original inhomogeneous linear differential equation is $y = C(x)x^2 = (x+k)x^2 = x^3 + kx^2$. It can be shown that this solution satisfies the original equation."

[Method 2]: Integral factor (the textbook method)

Still using the above example Dr.C says: "Textbooks teach the integral factor formula. I would like to introduce a *step by step* procedure in applying the formula. Compare the above equation $\dfrac{dy}{dx} - \dfrac{2}{x}y = x^2$ with the general form equation $\dfrac{dy}{dx} + p(x)y = q(x)$, we know that $p = -\dfrac{2}{x}$ and $q = x^2$. Therefore:

$$p = -\dfrac{2}{x}$$

$$q = x^2$$

$$\int p\, dx = \int -\dfrac{2}{x}\, dx = -2\ln|\,x|$$

$$e^{\int p\,dx} = x^{-2}$$

$$e^{-\int p\,dx} = x^2$$

"The solution of the linear differential equation is

$$y = e^{-\int p\,dx}\int q(x)e^{\int p\,dx}dx = x^2\int x^2(x^{-2})dx = x^2\int dx = x^2(x + k)$$

"When you apply the integral factor method, go step by step, write down p , q , $\int p\,dx$, $e^{\int p\,dx}$ and $e^{-\int p\,dx}$ one after another in order, then substitute them into the formula $y = e^{-\int p\,dx}\int q(x)e^{\int p\,dx}dx$. This method can be compared to the first method (converting the integral constant C into a function $C(x)$). Knowing both methods helps you understand linear differential equations better."

Students are eager to try both methods to solve linear differential equations.

Final words

Spring is here. Outside the window cherry flowers bloom, birds cheep on the branches of trees, happy butterflies dance around.

At the end of the class everybody feels that she or he has learned many new methods from this learning center. Students say: "We study *every* section in a simple, interesting and easy way. We learn not only the math knowledge, but also the philosophy, the tips, the great ideas, and the new ways to approach problems. We will never forget the special methods learned here from Dr.C, from this learning center."

"I am so glad to have presented you a gift in every lesson --- **converting hard to easy,**" says Dr.C. "I believe you will love the happy time you spent in this place and remember the essence of learning. You will remember the philosophy that **'simple is beautiful'**. Now, my friends, let us put down our pens, walk outside the classroom to enjoy our life, embrace the beautiful Mother Nature, smell the spring and dance to celebrate your great success!"

(The End)